Attainment's
mental fitness

INSTRUCTOR'S GUIDE

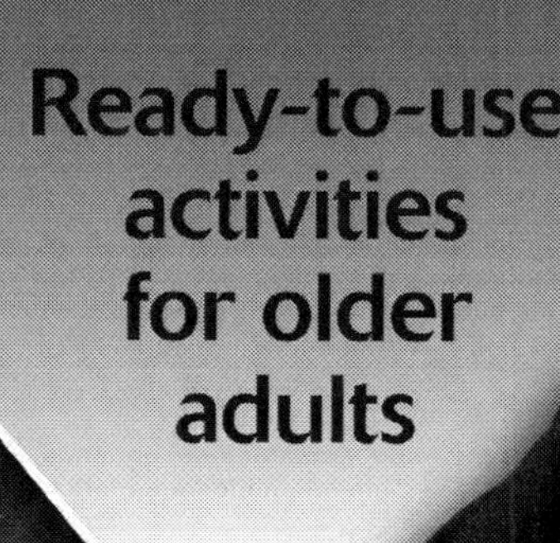

KARI BERIT GUSTAFSON

Win/Mac CD

This CD contains a printable PDF of the entire book.
You can review and print pages from your computer.
The PDF (portable document format) file
requires Acrobat Reader software.

If you have Acrobat Reader already on your computer,
open the file MentalFitness.pdf from the CD.

To Install Acrobat Reader:
Windows: Run ARINSTALL.EXE on the CD.
Mac: Run Reader Installer on the CD.

After installation, run Acrobat Reader and
open the file MentalFitness.pdf from the CD.

By Kari Berit Gustafson

Edited by Tom Kinney and Elizabeth Ragsdale

Graphic design by Elizabeth Ragsdale

ISBN: 1-57861-551-8
An Attainment Publication

Attainment Company, Inc.
P.O. Box 930160
Verona, Wisconsin 53593-0160
1-800-327-4269
www.AttainmentCompany.com

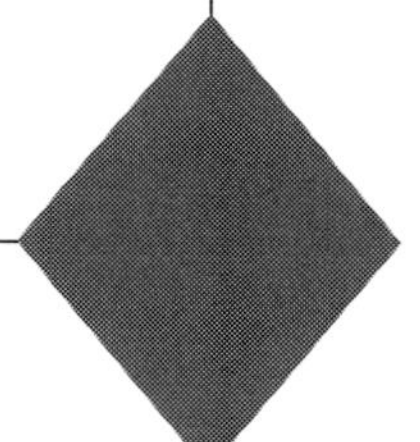# contents

about the author

Kari Berit Gustafson has focused her life's work on a celebration of aging for almost 20 years. Her original research looked at teaching older adults and enriching activity programs for them. That led to her work as an Elderhostel director, assisted living facility manager, tour guide, consultant, and internationally sought-out trainer and speaker on aging issues. In an era when showing any signs of age is frowned on, Gustafson has built a reputation for talking about this taboo topic with humor, intelligence and insight—and without condescension.

Gustafson has a BA in psychology and international health care from St. Olaf College and an MS in continuing and vocational education from the University of Wisconsin. She served as resident manager, director, and assisted living manager in senior housing facilities for more than a dozen years, while also teaching and directing programs for older adults. In addition, she has been a Life Enrichment activity program consultant for long-term care communities. Most recently, Gustafson has added caregiver coaching to her offerings.

To exercise her own brain, Gustafson enjoys traveling, reading, writing and working on the house she shares with her husband, her dad and his wife, and three pets—Eli the dog, Spike the bird and Solveig the cat. Known for her outstanding singing voice, she sings in English and Norwegian for audiences here and abroad. She attempts to follow her own advice in managing stress, keeping physically and mentally fit, enticing loved ones to get out of their ruts and living life fully engaged.

You can reach Ms. Gustafson at:

> Age In Motion, Inc.
> 564 Frenn Avenue
> Red Wing, MN 55066
> 651-388-6789
> kb.gustafson@ageinmotion.com
> www.ageinmotion.com

acknowledgments

I have so many people to thank I will not be able to name them all. First on my list is Marge Engelman—for introducing me to this marvelous world of aging and mental fitness and for being my number one cheerleader. In addition, there are the numerous Elderhostels at which I've had the privilege of teaching the last 20 years, and where it must be said my students enriched my life more than I did theirs. Also there's the "Brown Bag Lunch Bunch" at Wesley Park in Janesville, Wisconsin, and the hundreds of participants I've taught throughout the years; they gave me so much energy and shared their experiences so freely.

Melinda Ludwiczak, former director of the Skyway Senior Center in Minneapolis, deserves thanks for suggesting I write this manual and for understanding the importance of including mental fitness programs in Minnesota senior centers. A big thank you to Katharine Sween, who listened with all the patience of a best friend to my doubts and my enthusiasm; my brother Steve Augustus for helping me with the poetry section and for understanding my work with aging issues; the staff of Attainment Company, who recognize the need for mental fitness programming for older adults (and who are marvelous people to work with); and my editor, Sarah Entenmann, for her relentless editing, support and humor.

I can't resist thanking my precious dog, Eli, for sitting on my lap when I needed to take a break. The staff of *Creative Forecasting* graciously allowed me to spin off ideas from articles I wrote for their magazine, and I'm grateful. Finally, a special thank you goes to my business partner and husband, Eric Ramlo, without whose support I could not do what I do.

Kari Berit Gustafson

preface

ental Fitness Aerobics came into my life shortly after I met author Marge Engelman at the University of Wisconsin, Madison. One of my courses was Introduction to Aging, held on Saturday mornings at 8:00, not my best time. But Marge had a wonderful way of inviting us to study the topic of aging, and soon we all wanted to talk about this too-often taboo subject, no matter how sleepy we were.

She had us envision ourselves as an 80 year old person. We were to sketch a picture of our physical selves, where we lived, who we were around and what we were doing. (This exercise is one I continue to use in my workshops, as it gets everyone to look into the future and stirs up a lot of laughter.)

By the time I met Marge, the myth "You can't teach an old dog new tricks" had become a hot-button topic for her. Her graduate work had already centered around creativity and older women. After working with a dynamic group of women in rural Wisconsin some years later, she rededicated herself to the topic. In her program, Marge gave group members "brain workouts," drawing on a variety of exercises that challenged them to use all their senses, especially memory, and to learn new ideas.

I visited her Belleville class and was inspired by these women—so full of energy and zest and humor. They worked puzzles, wrote poems and dissected art. After my visit to Belleville, I started a discussion group at an independent senior apartment I managed. My goal was to incorporate similar programs and see what happened. Most of the residents had high school diplomas, but some had dropped out after eighth grade to help on the family farm. One woman, who was legally blind, held a Master's Degree. At the beginning, I was pulling out information from them, coaxing them and coming up with all the ideas and activities myself. By the time I left Wisconsin, this group was exploring and writing Psalms, penning magic-tale narratives (complete with life lessons) and writing songs. They were engaged.

Collecting her various exercises and her research on the brain, Marge published her first book, *Aerobics of the Mind,* in 1996. She followed the book with a set of cards, *Mental Fitness Cards: Aerobics for the Mind,* published by Attainment Company in 2004. When I teach this course, I call it "Mental Fitness Aerobics: Creating a Health Club for the Mind," and it's one of my most in-demand programs.

Throughout my 20 year career teaching Elderhostel students and working in assisted living and senior housing, I have made it a priority to step up the level of programs offered participants. Even in dementia care units, I have successfully included mental fitness programming. This guide comes out of a need professionals in the field articulate—they want a well-constructed, ready-to-use mental fitness program. I hope you find it valuable.

introduction

the Mental Fitness Instructor's Guide is a timely, invaluable resource for activity directors, adult-day program directors, parish nurses, housing administrators, and family and loved ones. It is also a wonderful tool for nurses, aides, housekeepers, maintenance people and volunteers. Throughout this guide, I will show you how to use Marge Engelman's **Mental Fitness** and **Thinking Cards** in group sessions—formal or informal. I will also point out how you can use mental fitness activities at staff meetings, before discussion groups, after exercise groups, on the bus en route to events, as casual activities and as program boosters to support monthly themes. Whether you're interested in keeping staff engaged with residents or providing richer visits for family members and loved ones, this guide can greatly enhance brain fitness programs and give everybody involved in elder care a unified sense of direction.

The guide is set up in eight themes. Each *Theme* can be used as one session or split into two or more sessions. You can even use a Theme over the course of a month, presenting one or two activities at a time. How you use Themes depends on the following:

◆ *Your group's cognitive ability.* If you have a high functioning group and can hold their attention for 1 to 1½ hours, you may be able to work through a Theme in one session. A group functioning at a lower level might work through the same Theme over two or three sessions.

◆ *The number of people in your group.* The ideal group is 3 to 15 participants. It takes longer for a larger group to do the activities.

◆ *The space available for your activities.* It's always best to have a space with tables and chairs, good lighting and a door that closes, allowing maximum concentration. Just as important is that everyone can see and hear the facilitator. It is more difficult to conduct a mental fitness group in a living room setting, but not impossible. If that's the space you have available, make a circle to create a closed space and connect all participants. When picking a single activity to do on a bus en route to an event, it's vital to consider the restrictions your space imposes.

◆ *Your talents, interests and experience.* To be an excellent facilitator for older adults, it helps if you have unearthed your deep-down attitudes about the elderly and about your own aging. If someone in their retirement years has been a strong role model for you—particularly a parent, grandparent, aunt or uncle—your feelings about growing older may be positive. Unfortunately, the reverse is also true. Stereotypes in the media can also play an important part in how you perceive aging.

If, as facilitator, you are able to show a lot of respect for this age group as interesting and intelligent people, they will feel comfortable participating in these activities and you will have an easier time forming a productive, cohesive group. Everyone will have more fun!

Structure of the Guide

Each Theme is laid out in a similar format, but they don't all include the same number of activities. Don't feel you have to adhere to the suggested activities only or to the written script. Both provide you with a map to structure the activity and suggest what to say to your group, but they aren't meant to be rigid. I've also included instructions to prepare for the activity and pertinent information to share with the group.

The first page of each Theme includes:

◆ *Goal.* To help you understand and document, if necessary, the therapeutic value of the activity.

◆ *Cards needed.* The list includes both **Mental Fitness Cards** for healthy adults and **Thinking Cards** for adults with mild cognitive impairment (MCI) or early stage dementia. If you have either or both decks of cards, pull those needed before the session and tell staff, family, volunteers and participants what you'll be covering. This is a great way to encourage engagement and interest in the activity. Note that sometimes the Mental Fitness and Thinking Cards have identical titles. The difference is that Thinking Cards are easier to understand, and some contain fewer steps or directions.

◆ *Other resources.* This lets you know what reproducibles you will need in addition to the cards. It also tells you when to have props ready— for example, a melon is sometimes used to represent the human brain.

◆ *Supplies.* This list tells you to prepare pencils, paper, an overhead projector and so forth.

Cognitive adaptation

Cognitive adaptation refers to a person's thinking skills and abilities, including understanding and reasoning. While this guide was written for persons who are aging normally, reality dictates that we also adapt activities

for people with lower cognitive function. The Thinking Cards were adapted for people with MCI or a disease with a dementia component. When found here under the heading "Cognitive Adaptation," the Thinking Card replaces its identically titled Mental Fitness Card.

Homework

At the end of each Theme is a homework assignment. Use this as a tool to encourage participants to stay engaged in the Theme. I assign homework in nearly all sessions I teach. I find it gives some people a reason to dig deeper, ask more questions and return excited for the next activity.

Participant Materials—CD-ROM

At the end of each Theme are numerous helpful reproducibles. Either photocopy the pages or print them out from the PDF format files on the CD-ROM.

Mental Fitness Instructor's Guide DVD

Mental Fitness Program includes DVD.

Along with the book and the two sets of cards—available for separate purchase—we've included a DVD that shows the **Mental Fitness Instructor's Guide** in action. Viewing this video will give facilitators new to the field confidence in their ability to use this rewarding and simple-to-use program. On the other hand, experienced facilitators can discover how refreshing this new approach is.

For each Theme, the DVD shows participants doing three sets of activities. In addition, it demonstrates one whole Theme—the facilitator and participants do all the activities in that Theme. When no facilitator is available, although not the ideal scenario, the video can even be used to lead the group.

Using Mental Fitness and Thinking Cards

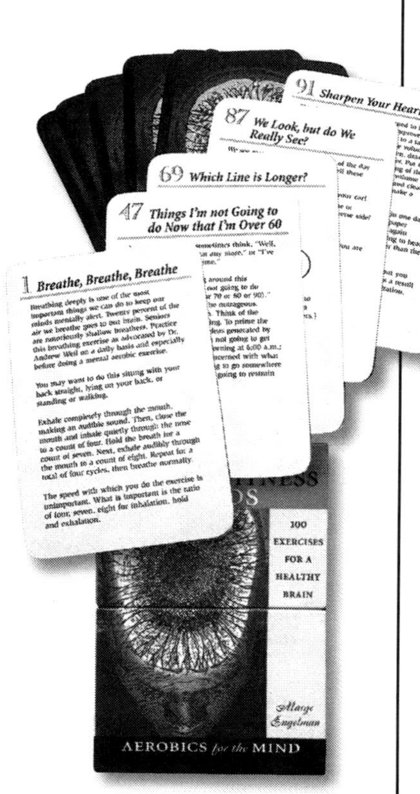

Having the **Mental Fitness** or **Thinking Card** decks allows you to incorporate the cards into your programs in many other ways. Listed are a few examples.

Pull card en route to event

For example, on the bus headed to an event, pull Mental Fitness Card 87 ("We Look, but Do We Really See?"). Once everyone's on the bus, grab the bus microphone and ask the various questions. When you've worked through all the questions, see if the group can come up with others. Steer the group away from excessive reminiscing by also asking about things seen every day. For example, "What's the color of your bedspread? Whose face is on 1, 10, 20, 50 and 100 dollar bills? What color pen do you use most often? What is your favorite time of the day?" And so on.

Use one-on-one

Once staff, family or volunteers learn how to use the cards, they can easily engage a participant. For example:

◆ If an older adult watches a lot of television, suggest they use Mental Fitness Card 4 ("Enhancing TV Watching") to help make their TV viewing experience more instructional.

◆ Pull Mental Fitness Card 40 ("Addition and Subtraction") and have a grandchild and grandparent work through addition and subtraction problems together. (The answers are shown on page 147.)

◆ Give Mental Fitness Card 28 ("Try to Remember") to a high school student and pair him or her up with an older adult. Have one read the first part of the card and the other finish it. Follow directions at the bottom of the card. (You may want to provide a copy of the card for each person so that they can write freely on it.) This presents a wonderful opportunity to look at self-esteem together.

◆ Encourage housekeepers and maintenance folks to take a card along as they go about their workday and to look for opportunities to engage a resident.

◆ Take along Mental Fitness Card 19 ("The Months of the Year") and work at reciting the months (you'll probably learn a tune or two from the residents); then try to recite them alphabetically.

Make adaptations

Tweak the activities in the card deck as necessary, depending on your group. For instance: You are using Mental Fitness Card 23 ("Pyramid Sentences") in a skilled nursing facility with participants who have difficulty writing. Use a white board and work the activities as a group, writing in bold letters. If some group members have poor eyesight, help them out by talking about a Theme, then telling them how many words you need next.

Start staff meetings with a card

Before a staff meeting, pull Mental Fitness Card 55 ("If You Were . . .") and go around the group, allowing each staff member to answer once, following this example: "If I were an animal, I would be a dolphin, swimming freely through the oceans and leaping out of the air. The three adjectives that describe me are playful, energetic and powerful." Staffers get only one minute to answer the question and describe themselves with three adjectives. No interruptions—others should acknowledge what was said, but not refute or challenge the staff member's feelings. Make sure everyone gets a turn.

Exercise brain after exercising body

If you regularly exercise the gray matter right after physical exercise, the group will look forward to it—and reap the benefits. Here's an example: Following physical exercise, give everyone a cup of water and then, using

Mental Fitness Card 10, have the group do the "Alphabet Stretch." With your group sitting in a circle, ask someone to name an animal that starts with the letter A. Work your way around the group, trying to let everyone have a chance. If you have someone in the group who finds this activity difficult, let others pull him or her along. Try not to let one person, however, monopolize the group. You, as the leader, are the encourager—be positive and help fill in gaps when necessary. If the group is high functioning, make the activity more challenging by choosing exotic foods or animals.

introduction
Participant Materials

We Look, but Do We Really See?

Mental Fitness Card 87

We see many things in the course of the day, but do we REALLY see? Ask yourself these questions:

- What color is the upholstery in your car?

- Which coin—a penny, nickel, dime or quarter—has a building on the reverse side?

- What color are the door knobs in your home?

- What is the design on the stamps you are using now?

- Describe the face of the person who delivers mail.

- What kind of trees grow in your neighborhood?

- What kind of wood is used in your furniture?

Now devise your own list of questions and ask them of a family member or friend.

Enhancing TV Watching

Mental Fitness Card 4

We are told that when you watch TV, the brain waves are similar to when you are asleep. We also know the typical older adult watches 43 hours of TV a week. So, what can we do to make TV watching more challenging to our brains? Try several of these ideas today and often.

- Play Jeopardy or Wheel of Fortune or other TV games.

- Watch the news and when the program is over, recall the topics covered.

- If you are listening to an interview, count the number of times the speakers say um-m-m.

- Listen for words that are unfamiliar and after the program, look them up in the dictionary.

- Take note of the clothes people are wearing and list suggestions for improving their appearance.

- If you watch the advertisements, challenge yourself to develop a new ad for the product.

Addition and Subtraction

Mental Fitness Card 40

Place a + (plus) or a – (minus) sign between the digits so that both sides of each equation are equal.

3	2	1	4	1	3	=	10
8	7	1	4	4	6	=	4
5	3	2	4	1	5	=	14
2	1	8	9	3	5	=	20
5	3	4	4	2	9	=	9
7	6	2	9	9	3	=	0

If you like this activity, invent some of your own.

Try to Remember

Mental Fitness Card 28

"Our deepest fear is not that we are inadequate. Our deepest fear is that we are powerful beyond measure. It is our light not our darkness that most frightens us. We ask ourselves, who am I to be brilliant, gorgeous, talented and fabulous? Actually, who are you not to be? You are a child of God. Your playing small doesn't serve the world . . . As we let our light shine, we unconsciously give other people permission to do the same . . ." Adapted from a speech by Nelson Mandela.

Underline the important words in this speech. Write a headline that portrays the meaning of the words. Decide on a tune and sing the words to it. Read them aloud. Now put aside the words and write as much as you can remember. Did you surprise yourself at how well you did?

The Months of the Year

Mental Fitness Card 19

Recite the months of the year in chronological order. Now, try to recite the months in alphabetical order.

You will probably find the alphabetical listing more difficult since we almost always recite the names of the months in chronological order.

Try first to say them without writing them. If that doesn't work for you, write them in alphabetical order.

Pyramid Sentences

Mental Fitness Card 23

Challenge yourself to develop a pyramid sentence. A pyramid sentence is one in which each word in the sentence has one more letter than the word preceding it. The sentence must be grammatically correct and must make sense. Try for at least five words in the beginning, and then try for seven or eight words or more as you gain experience and confidence. Since there are few one-letter words, it is all right to begin with a two-letter word. Here are several examples:

He
was
gone
after
dinner.

It
was
cold
since
winter
arrived
suddenly.

If You Were . . .

Mental Fitness Card 55

Answer each of these questions, preferably in writing, explaining why for each one.

- ◆ If you were an animal, what animal would you be?

- ◆ If you were a color, what color would you be?

- ◆ If you were a musical instrument, which would you be?

- ◆ If you were a flower, which kind would you be?

- ◆ If you were able to live anywhere in the world, where would you live?

- ◆ If you were a holiday, which one would you be?

- ◆ If you were an article of clothing, what would you be?

- ◆ If you were a kind of candy, which kind would you be?

- ◆ If you wrote a book, what would the title be?

Now, review your answers and decide on at least three adjectives that describe the kind of person you are.

Alphabet Stretch

Mental Fitness Card 10

Down the left-hand margin of a piece of paper, write the letters of the alphabet, A–Z, a different letter on each line.

Beside each letter, write a word that begins with that letter that is related to travel. For example:

A—airplane
B—baggage
C—car

If travel isn't your cup of tea, substitute words related to where you live or words related to families or words related to gardening. The idea is to stimulate the growth of dendrites in your brain to help keep it healthy. You may get stuck on q's and x's and z's, but keep trying.

one

Opening Your "New Brain"

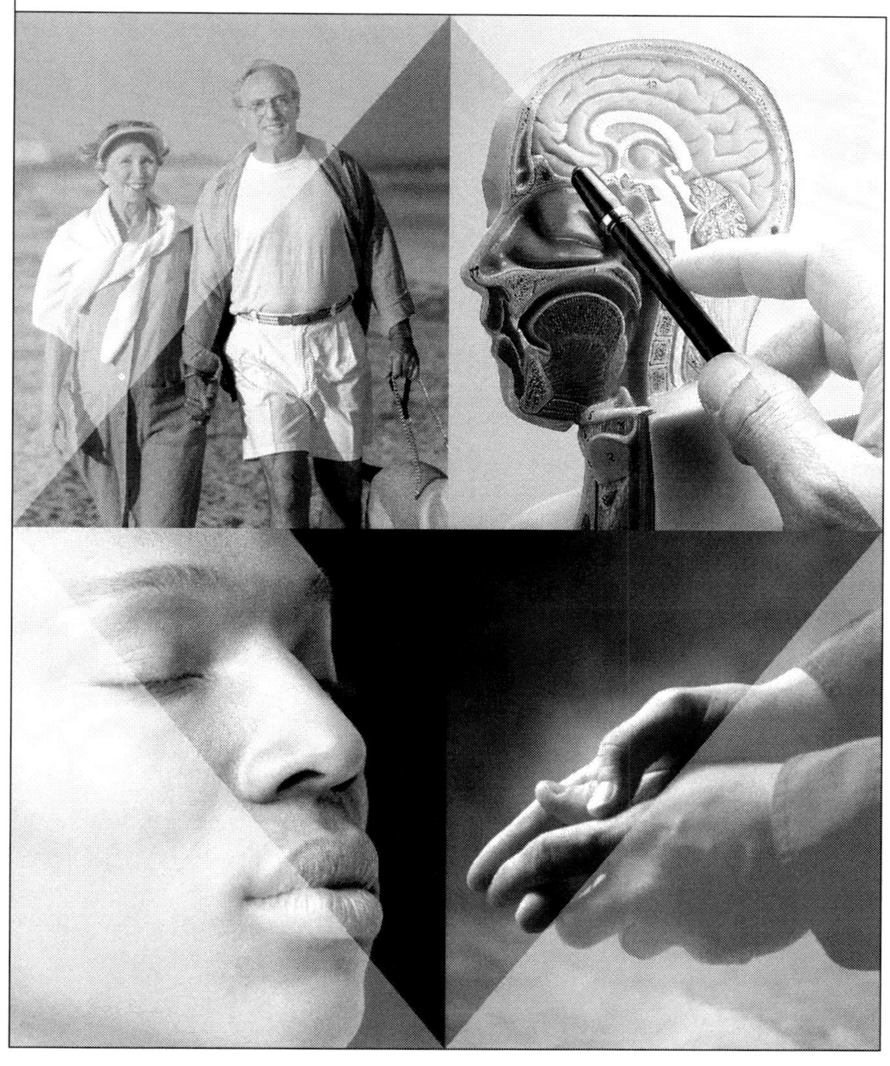

one

Opening Your "New Brain"

Goal	To open your participants' "new brains" by getting them out of their usual ruts. This is a great program with which to begin brain aerobics. Don't worry about explaining the new program to them at this point. Instead, focus on habits and ruts.
Cards needed	Mental Fitness Cards 1, 2, 8, 68, 86, 88, 89 Thinking Cards 6, 11
Other resources	Illustration of a neuron and optical-illusion pictures (Mental Fitness Cards 86, 88, 89), enlarged or prepared for overhead projector.
Supplies	Paper, pens/pencils, writing surfaces, overhead projector or bulletin board.

Before you begin

Distribute copies of "Your Brain Quiz" or enlarge it on the overhead screen. Invite participants to work on the quiz as the group is assembling.

Pertinent information

Begin by inviting your group to "Open your 'new brain,' which means setting aside the rote response, 'I can't do this; this won't work for me.' Help defy the myth that older adults are unwilling to change. By opening your new brain, you listen to ideas with the attitude, 'I wonder what I'll learn from this information and how it could benefit me.'"

So many times we prejudge an event before it even begins. Some of this has to do with fear of the unknown, and some is our fear that we won't be able to keep up. If you help your group bring out their fears beforehand, it will make the session go more smoothly. Simply take a white board or flip chart and ask the group, "What have you heard about learning in older age?" Then move into answering "Your Brain Quiz."

Separating fact from fiction

Take a look at "Your Brain Quiz," and work through the questions, providing the facts behind the myths. Keep in mind that this quiz is about normal aging, rather than aging with disease.

Your Brain Quiz

1. *After about age 40–50, you can expect your mental powers to decline.* **FALSE.**

   Quite the contrary. There is now evidence that the brain grows stronger, even physically larger, with regular use and purposeful exercise.

2. *Memory loss is a natural part of the aging process.* **FALSE.**

   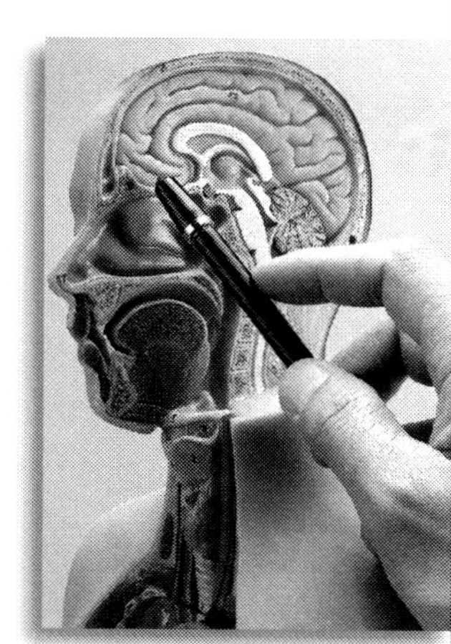

   The truth is that your memory can actually improve with age. Ask the participants, "How many of you forget? And when you can't remember something, you say, 'I must be having a ___________.'" (They usually fill in "senior moment.") Follow that with, "How many of you know teenagers who forget things? Or how about kindergartners? They leave behind mittens, lunch boxes, boots, etc." Then I add, "And I often forget and I'm forty-something; on what do I get to blame my forgetfulness? The truth is that as we age, we lose some ability to quickly recall facts, names or numbers, what we call *fluid intelligence*. Not having something on the tip of your tongue doesn't signal Alzheimer's Disease. As we get older it becomes more difficult to multi-task, but having become much wiser as we age, we now realize we don't *need* to do two things at once! Wisdom—or 'crystallized intelligence'—grows with age. We have a much richer foundation of experiences and knowledge from which to make decisions. It may take more time. To that I say, 'Big deal.' We could all benefit from slowing down a little."

3. *Chronic confusion and forgetfulness are the first symptoms of approaching senility.* **FALSE.**

   Explain to your group, "More often than not these symptoms can be traced to a vitamin, mineral or dietary deficiency. I have witnessed a number of 'confused' older adults become 'un-confused' once their medications were straightened out. Forgetfulness can be a symptom of a physical or emotional problem. Many older adults forget more and are increasingly confused when they have to move into an assisted living or nursing home. When something changes drastically, life becomes more stressful. Stress can cause many people to forget. There is a difference between forgetting where we put our car keys (normal forgetfulness at any age) and not knowing what car keys are or what they do (a warning sign of dementia).

4. *There is nothing you can do to slow the aging of your brain.* **FALSE.**
   There is a great deal you can do to keep your brain and mind going strong. Doing brain aerobics is one way.

5. *Once dendrites are lost, they cannot be regenerated.* **FALSE.**

New research is showing that dendrites can be regenerated. When giving this answer, I often say, "And what are dendrites anyway?" This question gives you a wonderful opportunity to present "A Look at Neurons" (page 13). Explain that dendrites are the tentacle-like fibers, at the end of neurons, that carry impulses to other cells involved in memory and learning. When you challenge yourself to learn something new, you're waking up those dendrites and they, in turn, reach out to make connections with existing or new neurons. Emphasize to your group that this is very exciting news: We can, in a sense, regenerate our brains!

6. *Creative ability cannot be developed in aging persons.* **FALSE.**

A number of studies show that creative tendencies can get stronger as we grow older. Brainstorming (discussed in Theme Three) is one way to foster creativity.

7. *Once your memory "goes," nothing can bring it back.* **FALSE.**

There are many methods for improving your memory. (Sprinkled throughout the sessions are activities that work on improving memory.)

8. *Males are more creative than females.* **FALSE.**

Women have just as much creative ability as men, and studies show that they may be *more* creative. If I've got men in my groups, I often ask the men what they think of this. Usually they answer "false."

Who's at risk for decline?

1. *The less-educated.* Many studies show that those with a higher education or those who are lifelong learners—always wanting to learn more—maintain a healthier brain. This is not to say that people with PhDs don't get dementia; rather, your risk decreases the more you challenge your brain. When we continually learn new things, we stretch our capacity to solve problems and think better.

2. *Couch potatoes.* When we're bored and disengaged from life, our brains tend to atrophy.

3. *Physically unfit people.* The old saying, "what's good for the heart is good for the brain," rings true. Pumping the blood and getting oxygen to the brain are just some of the brain benefits of physical exercise. Exercise also gets those endorphins going, which increases one's desire to be more engaged in life.

4. *Those without enough sleep.* Our bodies and minds need adequate down time and a good night's sleep to function properly.

5. *Those who have sustained head trauma.* If the brain has been damaged, the risk of dementia increases.

6. *The stressed-out.* Our brains don't work well when we're forcing them to work at a fevered pace. Have you ever become frustrated with yourself because you can't figure out the answer to a problem? And then have

you tried "racking your brain" or "pounding your head on the table"? Funny enough, the answer comes at 2 a.m., when you've finally let go and relaxed.

7. *Folks with a poor attitude.* Having a negative attitude about life shows you're focused on things you have no control over. By concentrating on how you respond to situations rather than bemoaning the bad stuff life inevitably throws at you, you keep your brain from spinning in negative circles.

8. *Alcoholics and smokers.* Both cigarettes and excess alcohol damage the brain and increase the risk of disease.

9. *Those stuck in a rut.* Rutted brains don't flourish. When we're stuck in ruts, we're not challenging our brains; we are simply on automatic pilot. So challenge yourself to sit at a different place at the table, or set the table using different plates. Drive home from church a different way.

Breathing exercise

Introduce the importance of good, deep breathing on Mental Fitness Card 1. I ask my groups, "Is anyone a singer? Singers know they need to breathe from their ___________." (The singers—and there always seem to be some—will fill in the blank with the word *diaphragm.*) Ask participants to sit up straight and take a deep breath. Then guide them in their breathing by saying: "Breathe in while I count to three; breathe out while I count to three." Continue to do this until they have established a comfortable rhythm. Let them know, "We'll talk more about breathing in the next session." (If you haven't introduced breathing yet, I would suggest taking a look at the video example on breathing. We will also take a closer look at breathing in Theme Two.)

The Small Cage Habit

Read "The Small Cage Habit" as an example of ruts:

> Once upon a time there was a very sad polar bear who was kept in a very small cage in the town zoo. When the sad bear wasn't eating or sleeping, she occupied her time pacing . . . eight paces forward and eight paces back again. Again and again she paced the parameters of her very small cage.
>
> One day the zookeeper said: "It's depressing to see this bear pacing back and forth in her confining cage. I shall build her a great open and elegant space so that she may romp with great freedom and abandon." And so he did.
>
> As the space was completed, great waves of excitement charged through the town, and finally the magic day came to move the bear to her new headquarters. The town mayor delivered a rousing speech, with a chorus of children screaming in anticipation.

Mental Fitness Card 1

The city marching band manifested a brassy bravado of sound that reached a crescendo at the glorious moment that the sad bear was ushered into her elegant new quarters. Whispers of curious expectation rose from the crowd as they watched the great beast frozen in the uncertainty of the moment. The sad bear looked to her left and to her right, and then she began to move . . . one step, two, five, eight paces forward and eight back again . . . again and again. To the shocked amazement of the crowd, she still paced the parameters of her old very small cage.

After you've read the story, ask the group these questions:

1. What kind of bear is the story about?

2. How many steps did the bear make as she paced back and forth in the cage?

3. Who decided to build a new space for the bear?

4. Who gave a speech at the celebration?

5. Where was the band from that played at the event?

6. What adjective is used to describe the bear?

Look at optical illusions

Enlarge the illusions on Mental Fitness Cards 86, 88 and 89 and hang them on the board or show them on an overhead projector. Follow the questions on the cards. Some participants will have seen some of these illusions; encourage them to help others.

Answer to Mental Fitness Card 88 ("Seeing Squares")

You should be able to see up to 30 squares, larger, smaller and in different configurations.

Answer to Mental Fitness Card 89 ("Picture Illusions")

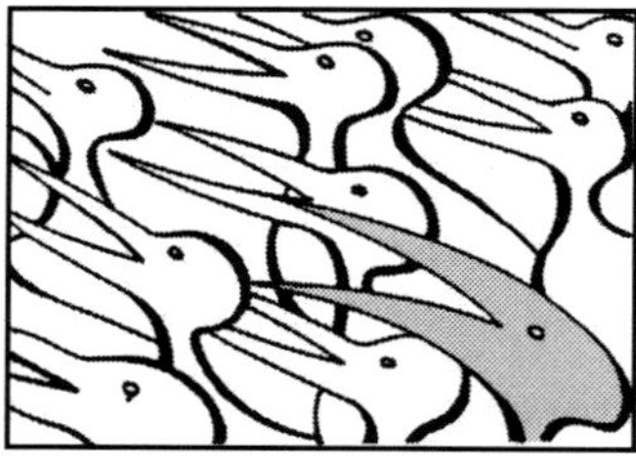

A bird or an antelope, or
you may see another animal.

What are your habits?

Researchers say it takes 21 days to form a new habit—and even longer to break one. Many of us don't know what our habits are. To get a clue to the habits and ruts we all have, fold your hands and arms in new ways:

1. Fold your hands with the fingers positioned between each other.

2. Look to see which thumb is on top.

3. Raise your hand if the left thumb is on top.

4. Raise your hand if the right thumb is on top. (Usually an equal number of participants go each way; there is no right or wrong way.)

5. Now try folding your hands the opposite way. (Often there is laughter, as many find it more difficult than they expected.)

6. Next, fold your arms.

7. Observe which arm is on top—right or left? (Again, the group is usually about equally divided for each position; some will observe that the left hand was on top, but the right arm was on top.)

8. Now try folding your arms the opposite way. (Again, generally there's laughter as people discover how awkward this is.)

Follow up by asking: "What does all this mean? We're not totally sure. It may have something to do with right/left brain tendencies. There is some suspicion that those who put the left thumb on top were originally left handed, but we don't know for sure. What this activity does show is that we get into ruts about how we do things."

COGNITIVE ADAPTATION

Use the instructions on Thinking Card 11 ("Fold Your Hands"). Don't worry about how participants do this; just remind them that it may feel awkward.

Analyzing daily habits

We all have beneficial daily habits and ones that aren't so helpful. Explain to your group: "We rarely analyze our habits and ruts, but let's take a look at some. List seven habits and use an asterisk to mark the ones you'd like to change." A list might look like this:

1. Before getting out of bed, I do some easy stretching.

2. I have morning coffee while reading the newspaper.

3. I turn on the TV to catch news, then start to doze—until mid-morning.*

4. I take the dog for a walk.

5. Then more coffee.*

6. I call a friend for lunch.

7. Then watch soap operas all afternoon.*

Now think about changing the habits that aren't beneficial.

Habit I'd like to change	*How I can change this habit*
Dozing in the morning.	Catch news on radio while getting dressed; wear headphones and listen to news while walking or cleaning.

Encourage participants to track their changes: "Write a list of ideas and options to make it harder to fall right back into that easy chair in front of the TV. On a calendar, mark each day you do something other than watch TV. Try for 21 consecutive days; but don't be hard on yourself when you suffer a setback."

COGNITIVE ADAPTATION

Talk about routines and tasks participants do each day. List them. Ask the group: "Which of these tasks feel good? Which do you like doing and which don't you like doing?" Make a worksheet with "Like to do" on one side and "Don't like to do" on the other.

Connecting the dots

Mental Fitness Card 68

This is a fun activity. Read the directions on Mental Fitness Card 68 aloud or have a group member read them. After the group has spent some time connecting the dots, ask them, "What restrictions have you set up for yourself in solving this problem?" Then reread the directions. Your goal is to get them to "draw outside the box." Be sure to show them the answer at some point. (This activity is also used in Theme Eight.)

Answer to Mental Fitness Card 68 ("Connecting the Dots")

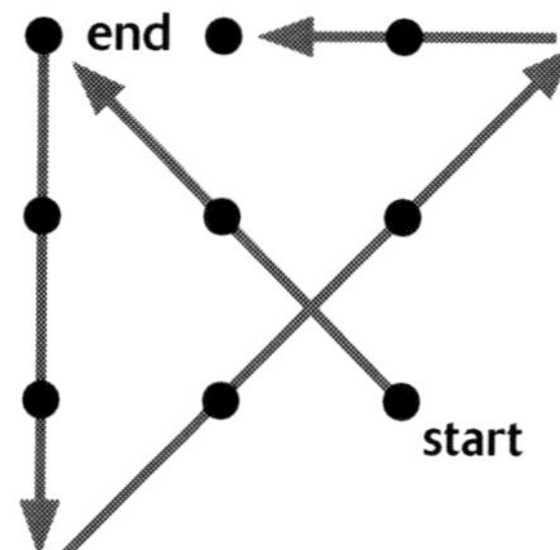

Mental Fitness Card 2

Homework

Send your group away with a copy of Mental Fitness Card 2 ("New and Different"), and encourage them to examine their daily ruts.

Thinking Card 6

COGNITIVE ADAPTATION

Give participants a copy of Thinking Card 6 ("New and Different"). They may need a partner for this activity, which is about trying new and different things. Encourage an aide, family member or volunteer to work with them.

ONE
Participant Materials

Your Brain Quiz

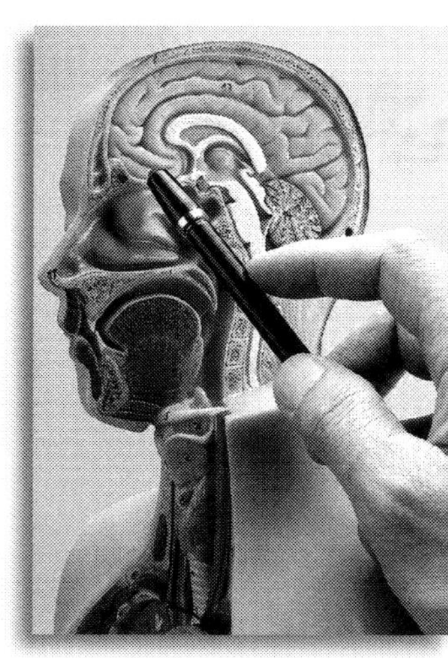

1. After about age 40–50, you can expect your mental powers to decline.

2. Memory loss is a natural part of the aging process.

3. Chronic confusion and forgetfulness are the first symptoms of approaching senility.

4. There is nothing you can do to slow the aging of your brain.

5. Once dendrites are lost, they cannot be regenerated.

6. Creative ability cannot be developed in aging persons.

7. Once your memory "goes," nothing can bring it back.

8. Males are more creative than females.

A Look at Neurons

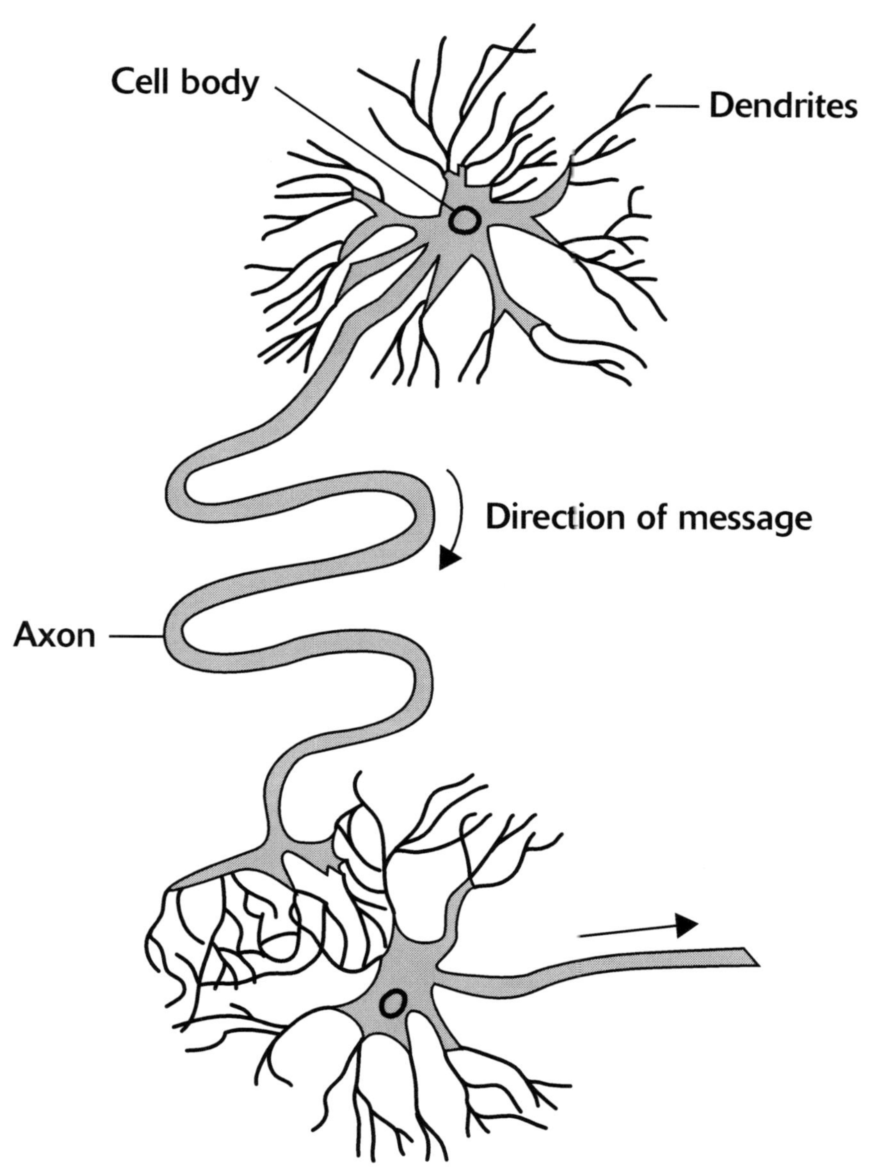

Who's at Risk for Decline?

1. The less-educated.

2. Couch potatoes.

3. Physically unfit people.

4. Those without enough sleep.

5. Those who have sustained head trauma.

6. The stressed-out.

7. Folks with a poor attitude.

8. Alcoholics and smokers.

9. Those stuck in a rut.

Breathe, Breathe, Breathe

Mental Fitness Card 1

Breathing deeply is one of the most important things we can do to keep our minds alert. Twenty percent of the air we breathe goes to our brain. Seniors are notoriously shallow breathers. Practice this breathing exercise as advocated by Dr. Andrew Weil on a daily basis and especially before doing a mental aerobic exercise.

You may want to do this sitting with your back straight, lying on your back, or standing or walking.

Exhale completely through the mouth, making an audible sound. Then, close the mouth and inhale quietly through the nose to a count of four. Hold the breath for a count of seven. Next, exhale audibly through the mouth to a count of eight. Repeat for a total of four cycles; then breathe normally.

The speed with which you do the exercise is unimportant. What is important is the ratio of four, seven and eight for inhalation, hold and exhalation.

Visual Illusions

Mental Fitness Card 86

What do you see in this image? What else do you see?
Can you see both at once?

What do you see in this image? Can you see the
old woman and the young woman?

Seeing Squares

Mental Fitness Card 88

How many squares do you see in this diagram? At first glance most people see 16 squares, then 17 if you count the outside square. Continue to look to see how many more squares you can find. We tend to get in ruts about how we see things. Look beyond the obvious.

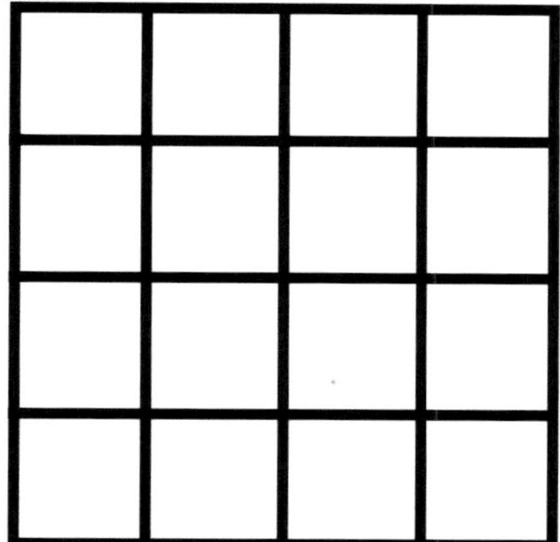

Picture Illusions

Mental Fitness Card 89

Is the figure in the lower right of each picture a bird or an antelope?*

*From Hanson (1958), found in Block and Yuker (1989).

Fold Your Hands

Mental Fitness Card 8

Fold your hands with the fingers positioned between each other. Now, look to see which thumb is over the top, the right or the left. Now, try folding your hands the opposite way.

Fold your arms. Observe which arm is over the top, right or left. Now, try folding your arms the opposite way. Most people find it awkward to fold their hands or their arms the opposite of how they ordinarily do it. The question is "why?" The truth is that we do not know for sure. It may have something to do with right brain/left brain tendencies. On the other hand, it may have more to do with habit and the way we have always done it.

List 10 things you do every day in exactly the same way, such as your morning routine or going for a walk. Think about how you might do those activities differently. Get out of the ruts! Do new and different things.

Fold Your Hands

Thinking Card 11

Fold your hands with the fingers positioned between each other. Now, look to see which thumb is over the top, the right or the left. Now, try folding your hands the opposite way.

Fold your arms. Which arm is over the top, right or left? Now, try folding your arms the opposite way.

Most people find it awkward to fold their hands or their arms the opposite of how they ordinarily do it. We don't know why that is—perhaps our brain is programmed to do it one way, or perhaps it is a long-held habit.

Connecting the Dots

Mental Fitness Card 68

Without lifting your pencil from the paper, draw four straight connected lines which go through all nine dots but through each only once. After you have tried two different ways, ask yourself what restrictions you have set up for yourself in solving this problem. Be sure to read these directions several times.

New and Different

Mental Fitness Card 2

Researchers are telling us that a good way to make the dendrites in our brains grow is to do new and different things.

Set a goal today of doing at least two things that are different for you. Here are some suggestions:

- When you set the table, arrange the plate, cup/glass and silverware in a different way.

- Fix your hair in a new way.

- Wear some jewelry you forgot you had.

- If you walk, take a different route.

- Phone someone you have never phoned or haven't called for a long time.

- Plan a surprise for someone.

- Visit a place you have never been before.

Think of some ideas of your own and set a goal of doing something new and different every day.

New and Different

Thinking Card 6

Researchers are telling us that doing new and different things is good for our brain. Our daily routine is important, but it is also good for us to do new and interesting activities. Set a goal today of doing at least one thing each week that is different for you. Here are some suggestions:

- Phone someone you haven't called in a long time.

- Visit a new place or a place you haven't been to in a long time. Examples are the zoo, a public garden, a restaurant, a museum.

- Fix your hair in a new way.

- Wear some jewelry or clothing you haven't worn in a long time.

- Help plan a surprise for someone.

two

Exercising Your Brain

two

Exercising Your Brain

Goal	To explain aerobics of the mind and to help participants understand that—much like our bodies—our brains need exercise to work better and become stronger.
Cards needed	Mental Fitness Cards 1, 7, 9, 18, 20, 28, 37, 43 Thinking Cards 5, 96
Other resources	Model of a brain or a 3-pound cantaloupe or honeydew melon, common straight pin, new standard pencil, playing card, penny, quarter, postage stamp.
Supplies	Paper, pens/pencils, writing surfaces, overhead projector or bulletin board.

Pertinent information

Ask your participants, "How many of you make a point of getting some form of aerobic exercise each week?" Ask them to raise their hand for every day, twice a week and once a week. "This is not meant to make anyone feel guilty; rather, it is just to see how many of us engage in physical exercise."

Now ask: "How many of you make sure to stretch out your brain each week? When was the last time you made a conscious effort to stretch your way of thinking, to try something totally new or do something creative?"

"The exciting news," you tell them, "is our brains are not hard-wired. Our brains have the ability to adapt, learn new things and accept change throughout life."

Aerobics of the mind are, simply put, stimulating and invigorating exercises for the brain. They were created by a teacher named Marge Engelman. She explains the thinking behind her invention (which you can paraphrase for your group): "The truth is that research on the brain is not advanced enough so that it can be said with absolute assurance that this or that activity will be the most stimulating. Undoubtedly, some day research will

have found which parts of the brain are stimulated by which activities. Perhaps it will be known how to regenerate neurons and dendrites in specific parts of the brain where needed. But until then, my tendency is to do a variety of activities that have potential for developing mental fitness." ,

Explain to the group: "Incorporating some simple brain exercises into your daily routine will help you prevent brain degeneration and make the most of your brain function. Wisdom grows with age; there is a special quality in people who have lived four decades or more. But your age group does need to exercise the brain sometimes." Remind participants that this type of exercise is something they do have control over: "It's not always in our control what happens to us, but we are in charge of how we respond." (I realize it's a different situation when someone has dementia; nonetheless, the brain can be exercised at any level of cognitive health.) "With a healthy brain, exercising it can go a long way toward keeping it in top form. When there is disease, exercising the brain won't necessarily help, but it won't hurt either."

Breathing exercise

It's always a good idea to include a breathing exercise as a way to warm up your brain. Ask your group, "How many of you breathe on a regular basis?" This usually gets a good chuckle, but it brings up a good point. We all breathe, but—too often—we hold our breath when we're under stress or we don't take in enough good, deep breaths.

Tell your group: "Twenty percent of the air we breathe goes to our brain. Seniors are notoriously shallow breathers. Good breathing is key to a good brain workout and important to your overall health." Andrew Weil, MD, and other experts on breathing indicate that the ideal pattern of breathing is to inhale as you count to four; hold your breath for a count of seven; then exhale as you count to eight. He indicates that it is not the speed with which you do the exercise, but the ratio of four, seven and eight for inhalation, hold and exhalation. Ask the participants to sit up straight and take a deep breath. Then guide them by saying: "Exhale completely through the mouth, making an audible sound. Then, close the mouth and inhale quietly through the nose to a count of four. Hold the breath for a count of seven. Next, exhale audibly through the mouth to a count of eight."

Repeat for a total of four cycles; then breathe normally. Dr. Weil says that he teaches this exercise to almost all patients he sees and receives reports of remarkable benefits. One of my participants suggested I tell people to "breathe in through your nose like you're smelling a rose and out through your mouth like you're blowing out birthday candles." Other groups have said they do similar breathing through yoga practice. Whenever participants share their experiences, it's important to listen and acknowledge their sharing.

COGNITIVE ADAPTATION

Use Thinking Card 5 ("Breathe, Breathe, Breathe"). Especially important are these simplified instructions:

1. Exhale completely through the mouth, making an audible sound (show the group).

2. Then, close the mouth and inhale quietly through the nose (again, show the group).

3. Hold the breath for several seconds.

4. Next, exhale audibly and deeply through the mouth (make noise while you're blowing out air).

Warm-up game

Let your group know that games have fostered aerobics of the mind exercise in both children and adults for generations. "I Give You a Cat" is one example of a mind-stimulating game. It is not about competition or receiving prizes. Often one or more people need some encouragement and help from other group members or the leader. This is okay and a part of the total process.

I Give You a Cat

Participants sit in a circle or around a table. The following questions and answers are addressed to the person on your right:

1. The first player says to the second: "I give you a cat."

2. The second player responds: "A what?"

3. The first player then says: "A cat."

4. The second player turns to the third person with: "I give you a cat."

5. The third player responds: "A what?"

6. The second player responds: "A cat."

As soon as the first player is finished speaking to the right-hand neighbor, she turns to the left-hand neighbor and says: "I give you a dog." The cat and dog messages are relayed around the circle; when they meet, that player must keep them straight and keep the conversation going. Eventually the cat and the dog will arrive back where they started. If you want to be really creative, substitute other animals—tiger and lion, cow and horse, gorilla and baboon, or any other pairing that comes to mind.

A look at your brain

Have participants hold a model brain. Or you can use a cantaloupe or honeydew melon that weighs approximately three pounds. (You can also

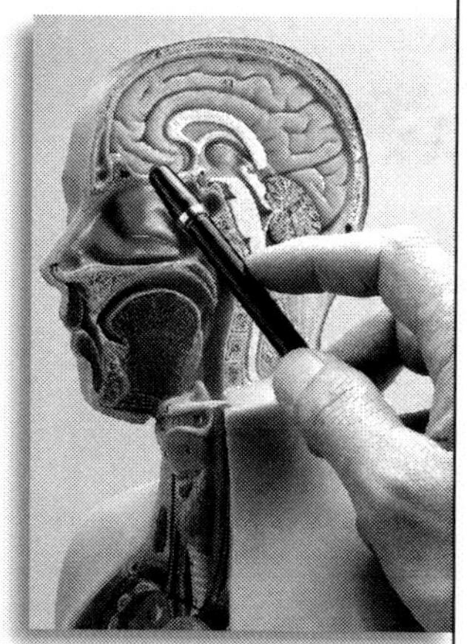

show the model of the brain on an overhead projector.) As participants hold the model brain or melon or look at the picture of the brain, share these facts with them:

1. The brain is made up of about three pounds of gray/pink jelly.

2. The brain is probably the most complicated piece of equipment in the universe.

3. Ironed out, it would be roughly the size of a sheet of newsprint.

4. To fit into the skull, it has to be highly convoluted.

5. The critical mass of the human brain is the cerebral cortex, the outer layer of the brain.

6. The cerebral cortex contains three-fourths of the neurons in the brain and is the seat of thinking, judgment, speech and memory (it is what makes us human).

7. The complexity of the human brain lies in the vast number of synapses (connections) between brain cells.

8. The number of interconnections among the cells is beyond the human imagination.

9. Researchers estimate that the normal brain has a quadrillion connections between brain cells, a number larger than all the phone calls made in the United States in the past decade.

Numbers, games and brains

Mental Fitness Cards
7, 37, 43

Stress to your group: "It is the process of working the game or puzzle that exercises the brain, not the winning or losing. It's also perfectly acceptable to work together."

Games Make Brains

Using Mental Fitness Card 7, ask the group: "What games do you remember playing as a child? What games do you play today? Do you play any games with your grandchildren?" (I fondly remember playing Parcheesi and Chinese Checkers with my Grandma Gladys.) Thinking about past games could be an excellent starting point for a game night or afternoon, where youth are invited in to play games. Wonderful games on the market include Scattegories™ and Rummikub™. Ask your participants to research new games on the market and to ask their grandchildren what games they're playing, other than video games!

Measuring Up

Use Mental Fitness Card 43. This is a fun activity that challenges your group to draw measurements, such as an inch, *without* measuring. It's helpful to have the objects handy—i.e., straight pen, standard pencil, etc.—to check the accuracy of the drawings. But again, I stress that the process, not accuracy, is what's important.

Story Problems

Provide a copy of Mental Fitness Card 37 to your participants. Research tells us that older learners do much better with information in front of them. Remind the group that these problems come from an 1892 arithmetic book.

Answers to Mental Fitness Card 37 ("Story Problems")

1. 7 pupils
2. 8,400 words
3. 20 oranges
4. 61 days
5. 150 minutes

COGNITIVE ADAPTATION

If the story problems are too difficult, try using Thinking Card 96 ("Counting Games").

Thinking Card 96

Hinky Pinky

I found this game in a book called *Games to Go,* by Jim Gladstone (Philadelphia: Quirk Books, 2004). Using three to five teams, this game challenges players to guess the answers to rhyming riddles. The game begins when someone on a team shouts "Hinky Pinky." That person then presents a clue that suggests a rhyming phrase consisting of 2 two-syllable words. For example: After a player calls out "Hinky Pinky," it is followed up with a clue such as, "It's a war among cows." A player from another team who knows the answer would say, "A cattle battle"—the correct response.

You might want to come up with other examples that get the juices flowing. The group will catch on, but sometimes it takes time. This isn't a serious game; it's total silliness. Pretty soon everyone will be groaning and laughing. And the game can go on and on, maybe even longer than you wish . . .

If a Hinky Pinky is 2 two-syllable words, then a Hink-Pink is 2 one-syllable words. A Hinkety Pinkety is 2 three-syllable words. For instance:

◆ Hink Pink: Clue is "It's a bird in the sand." Answer is "a dune loon."

◆ Hinky Pinky: Clue is "It's a cross between a pet fish and a pet dog." Answer is "a guppy puppy."

◆ Hinkety Pinkety: Clue is "It's an energy source that's full of praise!" Answer is "a flattery battery!"

As a further suggestion for Hinky Pinky, have your staff come up with clues and answers so you can act as host, allowing the teams to answer as soon as they get it (you could also use a format like *Jeopardy*). This would be a great way to involve other staff. In a monthly newsletter or mailing, invite family and loved ones to submit their Hinky Pinky ideas. Of course, you'll be the only one with the answers.

The power of words

Use the cards in the order 9, 20 and 18 so participants can understand with little trouble. Begin with proverbs, then move to reading upside down and finish by spelling words backwards.

Proverbs

I have used Mental Fitness Card 9 with various cognitive levels. Sometimes, I need to fill in more of the proverb, but usually someone knows it. Even if a "wrong" answer is given, praise the effort! In small groups, encourage your group to come up with 10 more proverbs.

Answers to Mental Fitness Card 9 ("Proverbs")

1. nine
2. is worth two in the bush
3. till tomorrow what you can do today
4. you have to have in your feet
5. but you can't make it drink
6. catches the worm
7. the heart grow fonder
8. in the eyes of the beholder (*or* as beauty does)

Upside-Down Reading

This is a fun activity using Mental Fitness Card 20. I often use the first paragraph of Mental Fitness Card 28 ("Try to Remember") for text to read upside down. Projecting it on a screen or handing it out, have the group read it first silently and then aloud. Tell them, "By reading upside down, you're not only exercising your brain, but also paying attention in a different way to the words you're reading."

Spelling Words Backwards

Use Mental Fitness Card 18. Choose a list of words from a newspaper. Start with four-letter words and write them on a flip chart or show them on the screen. Let the participants look at the word; then turn the flip chart to a blank page or turn off the projector and ask them to spell the word backwards. Follow directions on the card for further instructions. Tell them this is an excellent mind stretcher!

COGNITIVE ADAPTATION

Have the group work on spelling words, but don't push spelling backwards.

Homework

Invent your own proverbs. Read the newspaper upside down, increasing the length of time you can read. Play a new game with someone.

two
Participant Materials

Breathe, Breathe, Breathe

Mental Fitness Card 1

Breathing deeply is one of the most important things we can do to keep our minds alert. Twenty percent of the air we breathe goes to our brain. Seniors are notoriously shallow breathers. Practice this breathing exercise as advocated by Dr. Andrew Weil on a daily basis and especially before doing a mental aerobic exercise.

You may want to do this sitting with your back straight, lying on your back, or standing or walking.

Exhale completely through the mouth, making an audible sound. Then, close the mouth and inhale quietly through the nose to a count of four. Hold the breath for a count of seven. Next, exhale audibly through the mouth to a count of eight. Repeat for a total of four cycles; then breathe normally.

The speed with which you do the exercise is unimportant. What is important is the ratio of four, seven and eight for inhalation, hold and exhalation.

Breathe, Breathe, Breathe

Thinking Card 5

Breathing deeply is one of the most important things we can do to keep our brain alert and active. Twenty percent of the air we breathe goes to our brain. Seniors are notoriously shallow breathers. Practice this breathing exercise daily, as advocated by Dr. Andrew Weil.

Do this exercise sitting with your back straight, lying on your back, standing or walking.

- Exhale completely through the mouth, making an audible sound.

- Then, close the mouth and inhale quietly through the nose.

- Hold the breath for several seconds.

- Next, exhale audibly and deeply through the mouth.

- Repeat for a total of four cycles; then breathe normally.

A Look at Your Brain

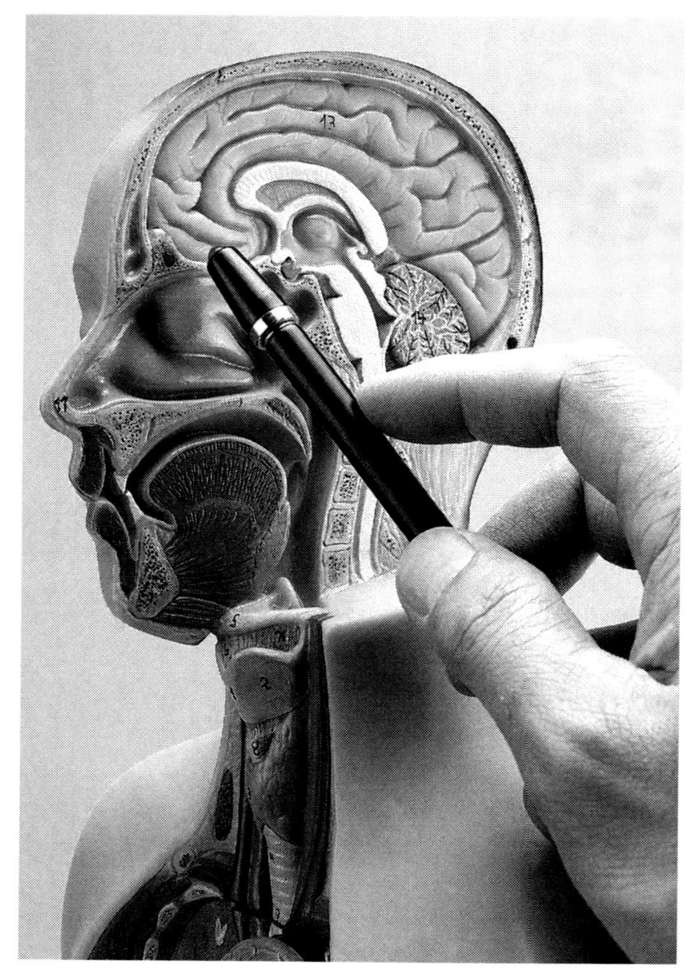

Games Make Brains

Many board games are mentally challenging. Do you have a game of Parcheesi, Chinese Checkers, Monopoly, Scattergories, Scrabble, chess, checkers or dominoes?

If you have one or more of these, find them and ask someone to play with you. You may have forgotten some of the rules, but they will come back if you concentrate for a bit. If not, why not be creative and think up some of your own rules?

How about Pick-up Sticks or Jacks? Remember playing them when you were young? These are both hand-eye coordination games but are wonderful for stimulating parts of the brain that may not have been challenged lately. Look for them in antique shops.

Have fun!

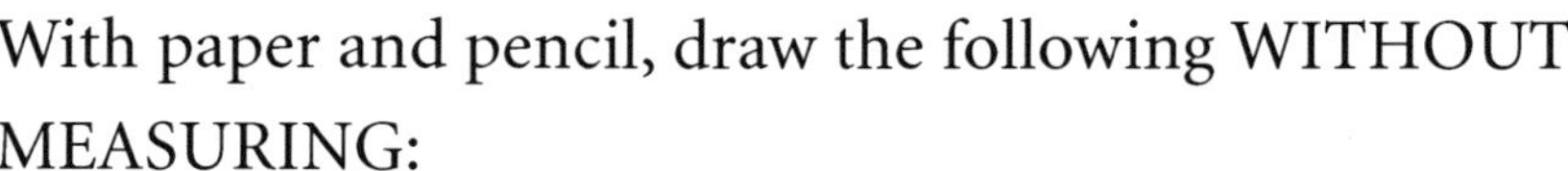

Measuring Up

Mental Fitness Card 43

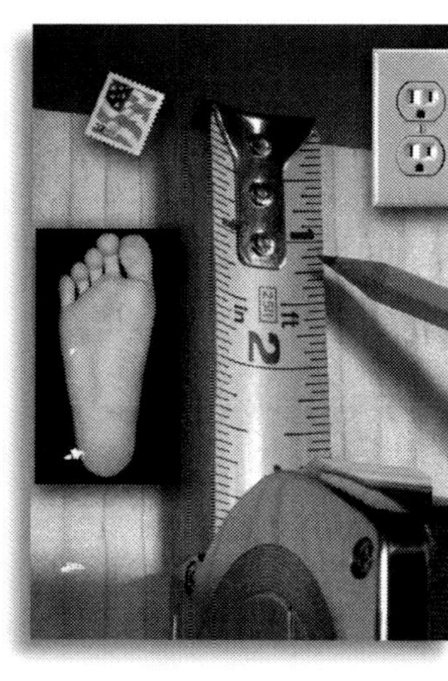

With paper and pencil, draw the following WITHOUT MEASURING:

- ◆ A line two inches long

- ◆ A line the length of an average common straight pin

- ◆ A line the length of a new standard pencil

- ◆ A rectangle the size of a standard playing card

- ◆ A circle the size of a penny

- ◆ A circle the size of a quarter

- ◆ A line the length of your foot

- ◆ A rectangle the size of a regular postage stamp

- ◆ A circle the size of an electrical outlet

Now compare your drawings with the actual objects to see how accurate your perceptions are.

Story Problems

Mental Fitness Card 37

Remember the story problems from your grade school days? These problems are from an 1892 arithmetic book.

1. If a school of 42 pupils were divided into 6 equal classes, how many pupils would there be in each class?

2. What is the estimated number of words in a book containing 24 pages, each page averaging 350 words?

3. How many oranges at 3 cents each should be given in exchange for 4 pounds of butter at 15 cents per pound?

4. How many more days are there in the months of March, April, May and June counted together, than in the months of September and October?

5. If you walked for 2½ hours, how many minutes did you walk?

Now that you have whizzed through these, develop some of your own story problems that are more challenging and try them out on family or friends.

Counting Games

Thinking Card 96

Do you remember when you learned your multiplication facts in school? You may have learned to count by twos, threes, fours, etc.

Try counting by threes:
3 . . . 6 . . . 9 . . . 12 . . . 15 . . . 18 . . .
How far can you go?

Now try counting by other numbers.

If you want a real challenge, try to list the prime numbers. (Prime numbers are divisible only by one and themselves.) To help you get started:
1 . . . 3 . . . 5 . . . 7 . . . 11 . . . 13 . . .

Can you continue?

Proverbs

Mental Fitness Card 9

With paper and pencil, complete the following well-known proverbs:

1. A stitch in time saves . . .

2. A bird in hand . . .

3. Never put off . . .

4. What you don't have in your head . . .

5. You can lead a horse to water . . .

6. The early bird . . .

7. Absence makes . . .

8. Beauty is . . .

Search your memory for at least 10 more common proverbs.

Now that you are "into" proverbs, invent several of your own.

Upside-Down Reading

Mental Fitness Card 20

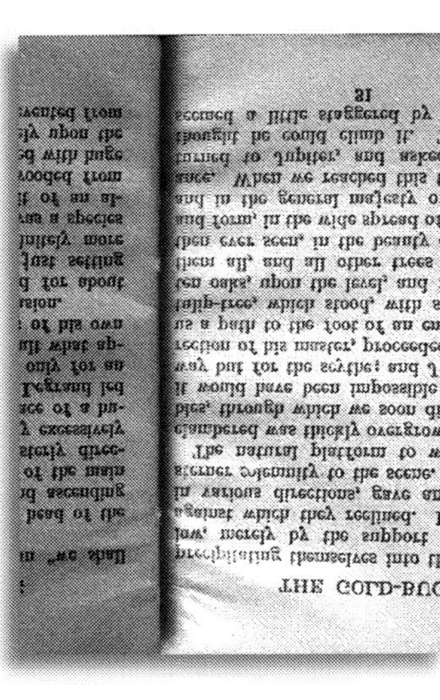

Choose an article from a newspaper or magazine. Hold it upside down and try to read it.

Since this is not our usual way to read, most people will have some difficulty doing this. It is a good exercise for the brain, however, as it struggles to make sense of the words. Speed is not a concern. Read as many sentences as possible until the brain feels challenged.

Do the exercises again tomorrow, and try to extend the length of time you can read upside down.

Try to Remember

Mental Fitness Card 28

"Our deepest fear is not that we are inadequate. Our deepest fear is that we are powerful beyond measure. It is our light, not our darkness, that most frightens us. We ask ourselves, who am I to be brilliant, gorgeous, talented and fabulous? Actually, who are you not to be? You are a child of God. Your playing small doesn't serve the world . . . As we let our light shine, we unconsciously give other people permission to do the same . . ." Adapted from a speech by Nelson Mandela.

Underline the important words in this speech. Write a headline that portrays the meaning of the words. Decide on a tune and sing the words to it. Read them aloud. Now put aside the words and write as much as you can remember. Did you surprise yourself at how well you did?

Spelling Words Backwards

Mental Fitness Card 18

The spelling bees of school days were oral exercises with two teams where the teacher gave each person a word to spell. This is a spelling bee with a difference.

Choose a list of words from a newspaper, magazine or book. Write down 5 four-letter words, 5 five-letter words and 5 six-letter words.

Beginning with the four-letter words, glance at the word and then look away and orally spell it BACKWARDS. Do this for each of the words you have selected. The more letters in the word, the more difficult. If this comes easily for you, try seven- and eight-letter words. This is a good mind stretcher.

three

Brainstorming and Discussing

three

Brainstorming and Discussing

Goal

To help your participants develop creative problem-solving skills so they become more engaged in life, are able to look at life issues creatively and refrain from closing themselves into a smaller world.

Cards needed

Mental Fitness Cards 45, 59, 75, 76, 77, 79, 80, 81
Thinking Cards 45, 54, 61, 63

Other resources

Paper clips; empty thread spool and metal can; enlargement of a picture, such as the picture on Mental Fitness Card 75, and another example or two of artwork.

Supplies

Paper, pens/pencils, writing surfaces, overhead projector or bulletin board.

Background

Brainstorming is a creative thinking procedure, not to be confused with barnstorming or brainwashing. It was invented by a creative person—Alex Osborn, founder of the Creative Education Foundation, in Buffalo, New York. Brainstorming is a simple procedure that can be used to stimulate creative thinking and problem solving. Its purpose is to generate a long list of possible solutions to problems. Since criticism or evaluation interferes with the generation of imaginative ideas, the thing to remember when brainstorming is not to evaluate the ideas until later.

The key ground rules for brainstorming are:

1. Criticism is ruled out.

2. Freewheeling ideas are welcome; the wilder the better.

3. Quantity is important; the more ideas the better!

Pertinent information

Tell your group, "In this day of nuclear energy, computers and hybrid cars, our world is changing very rapidly. The discoveries and innovations of the next 20 years will make changes in the previous 100 years seem snail-paced. We cannot foresee exactly what knowledge we'll need five or ten years from now to meet life's problems. We can, however, develop attitudes that will help us meet future challenges creatively. People who have developed creative problem-solving skills have an easier time making personal adjustments and meeting new challenges."

Some older adults have said to me, "Why should we learn to be problem solvers; shouldn't you focus on the next generation?" To that I say, "No, we need your years of experience and wisdom to help the next generations learn."

Brainstorming allows us to get rid of stale ideas. Remind everyone that when brainstorming:

◆ All ideas are welcome—there are no bad ideas.

◆ We're after quantity, not necessarily quality, at this point.

◆ Judgment of suggestions is unwelcome at this point (that comes later).

◆ You never know what can percolate out of a bizarre suggestion.

Be a strong facilitator in this process, keeping the group on task.

Brainstorming

Mental Fitness Card 45

Use Mental Fitness Card 45 to get the group ideas flowing. You can conduct this activity in the large group, while you take notes on a flip chart or overhead projector, or you can split into smaller groups and have participants choose a recorder and a presenter. Either is fine and depends on the size of the group with which you're working.

COGNITIVE ADAPTATION

Brainstorming is often misunderstood. Be sure to review the guidelines, and when working with a lower functioning group loosen them up a bit to make the instructions easier to follow. Leading a discussion group with people who have some dementia means that you, as the leader, need to be flexible. The discussion may not always follow a thread or make sense. Keep your sense of humor strong and go with the flow.

A brainstorming exercise

Mental Fitness Card 77

Use Mental Fitness Card 77 ("Paper Clips"). Begin by giving each participant a paper clip and instructing them to write the numbers 1–35 on a piece of paper. Next have them write down every use they can think of for a paper clip. Then throw out the obvious uses—like holding paper together—and encourage participants, individually or in groups, to move into crazy ideas of how a paper clip could be used.

Finding uses for "useless things"

Mental Fitness Card 76 ("Brainstorming—New Uses") can be used in a large group or in smaller groups. The goal is to be as creative as possible. Go for at least 30 new uses for empty thread spools and metal cans!

The Invisible

Mental Fitness Card 81 is a fun card to brainstorm with. Some responses can lead to a good discussion. For example, I once had a group tell me that love was *not* invisible (as the card says). Instead of arguing, I moved into brainstorming about how you can see love.

Breathing and stretch break

With all the creative juices flowing, it's time to stretch and breathe. Inserting a breathing exercise is always a good idea. Tell your participants: "Either standing or sitting, reach your arms up to the ceiling; then move them to the side. Shrug your shoulders like you're hugging your ears and release. Repeat this." Remind the group to "take in a good deep breath while counting to four. Hold for seven and breathe out for eight."

Group discussion

Brainstorming can easily be followed by a good discussion during which the group moves from being creative to using their analytical skills. While a stimulating discussion is a learning experience and a valuable social activity, it can easily get out of hand. All of us have been in a discussion group that hasn't gone smoothly. Inevitably participants wander from the subject; often one or two people dominate the discussion; sometimes everyone talks at once. Sometimes people argue. So here are some suggestions you can share with the group, saying in your own words, "As the leader, I will:

1. Sit in the circle with you.

2. Define clearly what our focus is.

3. Encourage everyone to participate, but also remind you that it's okay just to listen.

4. Interrupt gently if someone talks too much—to make sure everybody has a chance to share their opinions.

5. Help the group stay focused.

6. Remind you that silence and gaps in conversation are normal and a healthy part of a good discussion.

7. Explain that, although disagreement is expected and accepted, participants need to respect the opinions of others."

Along with setting forth these guidelines in the beginning, I suggest handing out a shorter version of the *Ground Rules for Discussion* used at the White House Conference on Aging in May 1995:

1. Each person's opinion counts.

2. Everyone participates; no one dominates.

3. One speaks; others listen.

4. It's okay to disagree, but not to be disagreeable.

5. Be positive.

6. Stay focused.

Brainstorming about wisdom

The goal of this session is to enhance self-esteem. Stand at the front of the room with a flip chart. Write down the ideas generated by the following questions (later post each sheet for referral):

1. What is wisdom? (Remind participants that there's no right or wrong answer.)

2. What makes a person wise?

3. When do you feel the wisest?

4. What is the most important thing you've learned about living?

When you've got four lists of ideas, move to a clean sheet of paper and as a group discuss the important elements of wisdom. The goal is to come up with a definition of wisdom. The definition may be summarized in a short, free-verse poem that uses the ideas generated by the group.

Pet peeves

Mental Fitness Card 79

Creatively and humorously look at Mental Fitness Card 79 ("Pet Peeves"). After you've created a list of them, come up with creative ideas (through brainstorming) about telling others they're bugging you. Don't let this get nasty; just have fun with it. As the group leader, you may need to set the tone by coming up with zany responses to someone's pet peeve.

COGNITIVE ADAPTATION

Thinking Card 63

Thinking Card 63 ("Pet Peeves") gives instructions geared especially for early stage dementia.

Title this picture

Mental Fitness Card 75

Using an enlargement of the picture on Mental Fitness Card 75, break into teams and have each group come up with titles. Set a time limit of two minutes; then have each group share their titles. (Although I don't usually recommend setting time limits for older adults, the purpose here is to set boundaries to start and end the brainstorming.) If you have another picture with you, mix up the groups and have them title it as well.

Imagining on your own

Mental Fitness Card 80

Give everyone an opportunity to do Mental Fitness Card 80 ("Imagining") on their own. Have them write down the numbers 1–20 and choose one of the ideas on the card, such as 20 things that can be put into a thimble. Give them one or two minutes.

Homework

Mental Fitness Card 59

Give everyone a copy of Mental Fitness Card 59 ("Creativity and Doodling"). Go over the card; then let them take it home with them, knowing they'll come to the next session and share their drawings.

COGNITIVE ADAPTATION

Thinking Card 54

Use Thinking Card 54 ("Creativity and Doodling"), if some participants
need suggestions of ideas.

Brainstorming

You are taking a bus trip that will continue for three days. The bus is very crowded. You are seated next to a person of the opposite sex, about your age or older, who has the same destination. This person talks constantly to you and even pokes your arm if you start to doze. You have two more days of this.

List as many ideas as you can for ways to deal with this problem. At least 15 ideas would be a good goal. When you think you have finished, press yourself to generate even more ideas. Remember to defer judgement. No idea is too ridiculous. Have fun in stimulating your brain to be creative.

Paper Clips

Mental Fitness Card 77

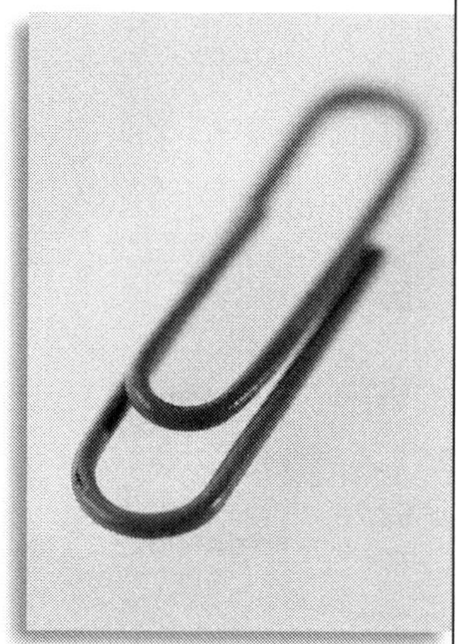

Write the numbers 1–35 on a piece of paper. Find a paper clip to look at and hold it in your hand. Now, write down every use you can think of for a paper clip.

The obvious uses, of course, are to clip things together. But, this activity is meant to stretch your imagination about NEW AND DIFFERENT uses. Be creative! You can unbend it and reshape it to foster new ideas. The possibilities are endless.

Paper Clips

Thinking Card 61

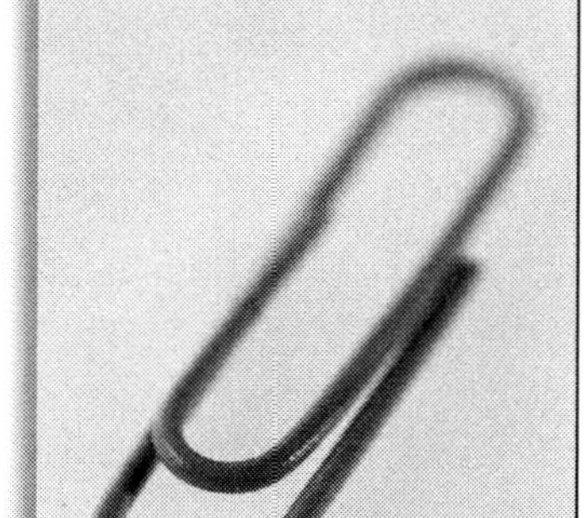

Find a paper clip, hold it in your hand and examine it.

Now, write down or say every use you can think of for a paper clip. The obvious ones, of course, are to clip things together. But, this activity is meant to stretch your imagination about new and different uses. Be creative!

You can unbend the paper clip and reshape it to help think of new ideas.

The possibilities are endless.

Brainstorming—New Uses

Mental Fitness Card 76

Brainstorming can be helpful in developing new uses for discarded objects. Try one or both of these challenges and go for at least 30 new uses for each.

- You have a sack full of empty wooden spools in your closet that you have saved for years, thinking that someday you will do something with them. List as many new uses for these spools as you can. Be as creative as possible.

- Many of us now recycle metal cans, but they have hundreds of interesting and unusual uses. List as many uses for these cans as you can, not limiting yourself to one size. You may use as many cans as you wish. It's okay to list crazy ideas, and the more the better.

The Invisible

Mental Fitness Card 81

List all the things you can think of that are invisible. Air, love, germs, thunder are just a few.

Try to list at least 30 invisible things.

If you get to 30, go for 50.

You Can Always Talk About the Weather

Thinking Card 45

◆ Do you remember any severe weather or storms? What happened?

◆ Do you think the weather has changed since you were a child?

Ground Rules for Discussion

1. Each person's opinion counts.

2. Everyone participates; no one dominates.

3. One speaks; others listen.

4. It's okay to disagree, but not to be disagreeable.

5. Be positive.

6. Stay focused.

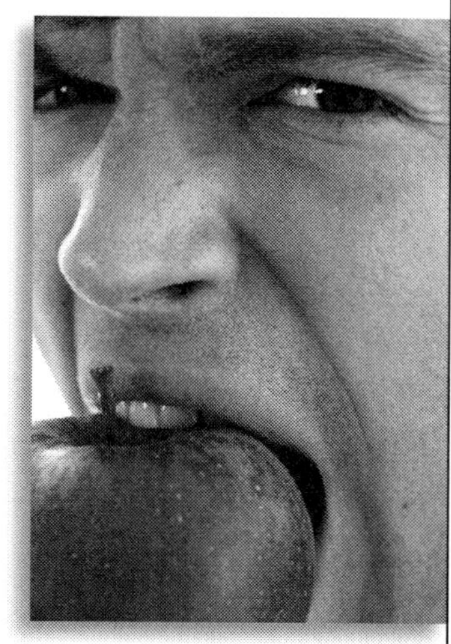

Pet Peeves

Mental Fitness Card 79

Everyone has pet peeves. Here are some examples: people who smack their gum, people who phone you and can't stop talking, or the advertising on TV.

On a piece of paper list one of your pet peeves.

Now, list all the ideas you can dream up as to how you might reduce this irritation. Try for at least 20 ideas.

Remember that in brainstorming, you let the ideas flow and go back later to decide which might be useful.

Pet Peeves

Thinking Card 63

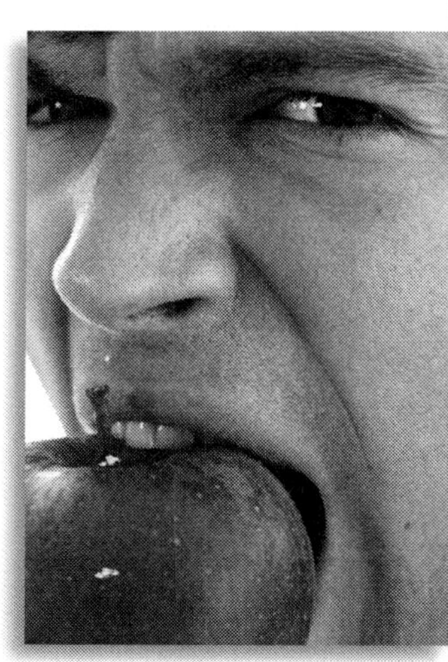

Everyone has pet peeves or things that are particularly annoying to them. Some examples are: people who smack their gum, people who phone you and can't stop talking, or advertising on TV.

Write down one of your pet peeves, or talk about it with a friend or family member. Then, brainstorm and list all the ideas you can think of that might help reduce your irritation.

To brainstorm, just let the ideas flow. Later, go back to decide which ideas might be useful.

Picture Title

Mental Fitness Card 75

Give this picture a title. Write it on a piece of paper. Think of at least 10 more titles and write them down. Now, pick the one that you like best.

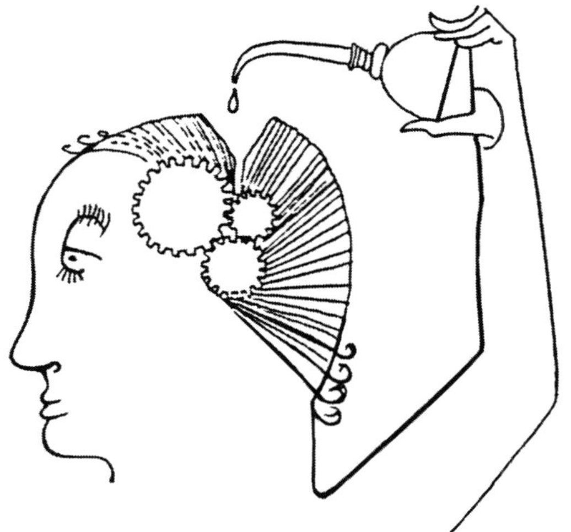

Imagining

Mental Fitness Card 80

Using paper and pencil, name as many things as you can that can be:

◆ put into a thimble

◆ hung on the living room wall

◆ used in cleaning a house

◆ used to dig up the soil

Try for at least 20 items in each category. Be as creative as you can, including unusual and different ideas.

Creativity and Doodling

Mental Fitness Card 59

What does this drawing look like? Think of as many different answers as possible. Now, take a piece of paper and begin to doodle. When you doodle, you don't have any particular thing in mind. You let your pencil just wander over the paper and see what happens. Try to keep your mind out of it, letting your imagination wander. Doodle for about five minutes. Take a look at what you have done. You may be surprised at how creative you have been. What is it? What could it be? Look at it upside down and sideways. It is a good brain exercise.

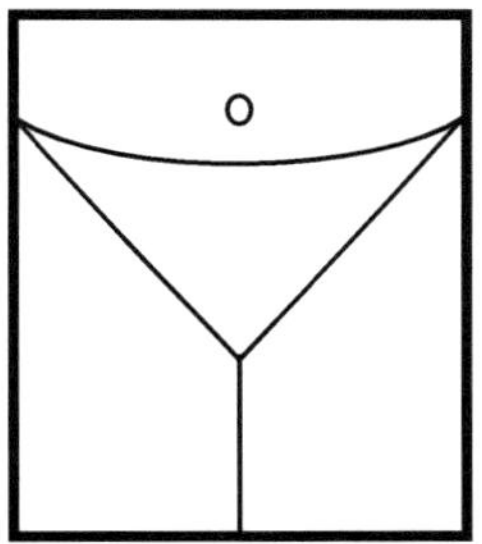

Creativity and Doodling

Thinking Card 54

What does this drawing look like? Think of as many different answers as possible. *What others have seen: bikini and belly button, an olive dropping into a martini glass, a lamp (upside down), an envelope, a suction cup.*

Now, take a piece of paper and begin to doodle. Just let your pencil wander over the paper without having anything particular in mind. Let your imagination wander, and see what happens. Doodle for about five minutes.

Take a look at what you've done. You may be surprised at how creative you've been. What is it? What could it be? Look at it upside down and sideways. It's a good brain exercise.

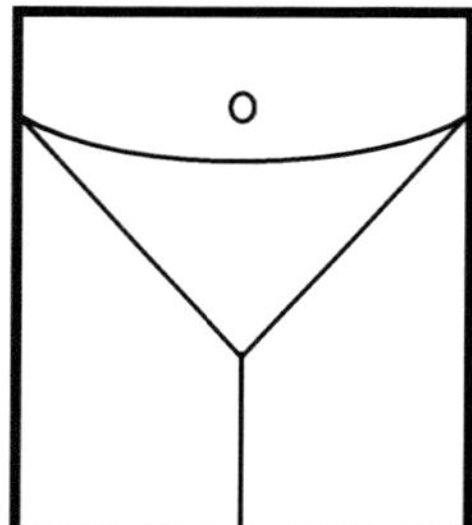

four

Going for a Walk with a Line

four

Going for a Walk with a Line

Goal	To exercise the right side of the brain; to present the role visual arts play in encouraging creative and active minds.
Cards needed	Mental Fitness Cards 61, 65, 66, 82, 90, 93 Thinking Cards 56, 57, 58, 66
Other resources	Variety of music recordings, favorite piece of art.
Supplies	Paper, pens/pencils, pencil sharpener, writing surfaces, overhead projector or bulletin board, tape or CD player.

Pertinent information

Creating and viewing art are stimulating activities, but they're something older adults may not do on a regular basis. Drawing and coloring are for children, aren't they? I say *no.* In this session we'll look at art that's appropriate for seniors and at the same time good for *anybody's* brain. Remind the group: "Open your 'new brain' and try something different." I don't draw often, but when I do, I sense that I'm using part of my brain that doesn't get enough exercise. Have fun with this session and let go!

Going for a walk with a line

Mental Fitness Card 61

Usually when you introduce drawing, someone in the group says, "But I can't even draw a straight line." A good response is, "Drawing straight lines is often a hindrance." Another will say, "I never was any good at art." You can assure group members that aerobics of the mind exercises have as their goal stimulating parts of the brain, not that of making fun of those without drawing skills. Give everyone an 8½ x 11 inch piece of paper and a pencil. It's always best to sharpen pencils beforehand, but keep a sharpener in the room for tune-ups. After you read the card, suggest that the group share a story and follow the process the card suggests.

Floor plan of your childhood home

Mental Fitness Card 65

Participants can do this activity with you or on their own. It demonstrates the ability to "remember through your hands." If drawing the whole house is too much work, tell them to choose a room. (For instance, I have no trouble at all remembering my childhood bedroom.) After you've all completed the activity, encourage participants to share their drawings. Pair the participants off and give them time to exchange ideas. You can also encourage them to compare their childhood home to later homes. Ask them: "Have you carried over any similar themes (bed positioning, window treatments, number of floors, artwork, inherited furniture, etc.)? In what room has a certain piece of artwork hung?" This activity promotes nostalgia and excitement.

COGNITIVE ADAPTATION

Thinking Card 57

The instructions on Thinking Card 57 ("Rooms in Your Childhood Home") are easier to follow when participants' dementia is early stage. Remind them: "It doesn't matter if the drawing looks correct—it's the experience of doing the work that matters."

Finish the line drawings

Mental Fitness Card 66

Make sure you've copied Mental Fitness Card 66 before this session. Put a copy of the worksheet on the overhead projector or flip chart so the group can watch you lead by example. It's a good idea to give the participants at least two copies of the worksheet so when they get the hang of it, they can develop more creative ideas on their own time and bring them to the next session.

COGNITIVE ADAPTATION

Thinking Cards 56, 58

Thinking Card 58 ("Cut It Out!") and Thinking Card 56 ("Tree People") provide alternatives to abstract line drawing. "Cut It Out" emphasizes cutting pictures out and tracing the lines, so you'll be stimulating the coordination between brain and hand. "Tree People" is a little more abstract. I would encourage you to help participants begin their drawings, as some may not remember what a tree looks like. You could put up examples of trees on the bulletin board or wall before you start.

Breathing break

It's always a good idea to insert a breathing exercise. Remind the group to breathe in for 4, hold for 7 and exhale for 8, and to "breathe in through your nose like you're smelling a rose, and breathe out through your mouth like you're blowing out birthday candles."

Shared doodling

This can be done in pairs or in several small groups. Have one person begin by doodling; then pass the paper to the next person. Tell them, "The point is to let your mind wander. Try not to think too much, but just let ideas flow." You may have to remind them throughout the session "not to think too hard." Simply repeat that they should let their hearts draw, not their minds. Each time the paper is passed from one person to the next, the lines need to be connected. But the end result doesn't have to look like anything specific. When all the doodles are completed, show the pictures and have folks imagine what the drawing *could* be.

Draw what you hear

Mental Fitness Card 93

Pick varied pieces of music, or better yet, have several of your participants choose a variety of pieces. I encourage you to stretch participant comfort zones by having them listen to music they wouldn't choose on their own, including "what the kids listen to today." Let them know it's important to "expand your minds and *really* listen to what you hear." The key is to play only part of a song; you don't want participants to tune out. I have had wonderful success playing different types of music, even rap. Remind them that the goal is "to stretch your minds and draw what you hear." As with anything, don't overdo it. Try a little new music mixed with music they prefer. This easily turns into a fabulous intergenerational activity. With grandkids on board, let participants show and talk about their drawings.

What to look for in works of art

Mental Fitness Card 82

This is one of my favorite activities. The instructions on the card say to find a well-known piece of art. To that I would add, "Find a piece of art by an artist who interests you." I often choose Norwegian art because of my interests. It's extra fun for me to have participants look at art I know a little about. Likewise, if they have artwork they know well, they get a real kick out of sharing it with the group.

Add questions and answers as the session moves along. One of my best experiences looking at art was in a dementia unit. We were a group of about seven looking at a picture of a small bowl of fruit. I was surprised by one man's comment about the knife in the picture disturbing the whole picture. There was no knife in the picture, but I didn't point that out. Instead, I asked, "Why don't you like the knife?" He explained, and then the whole group discussed it. As I left the room, they were still discussing the knife!

I also ask questions like: "What was the artist thinking when he or she was painting this? What mood were they in?" If there are people depicted in the art, I ask, "What do you think the story is with these people?" Any drawing or painting can be discussed. Use your imagination.

COGNITIVE ADAPTATION

Use Thinking Card 66 ("What to Look for in Works of Art"). As I've learned on dementia units, you really need to go with the flow. I'm always amazed at what some people see. The best part is that no one is wrong.

Homework

This is a fun activity folks can do on their own, then bring to the next session. Make sure you provide them with a copy of Mental Fitness Card 90 ("A Picture Takes the Place of a Word") so they have an example. You could also suggest they write a letter to their grandchildren using pictures instead of words.

four
Participant Materials

Going for a Walk with a Line

Mental Fitness Card 61

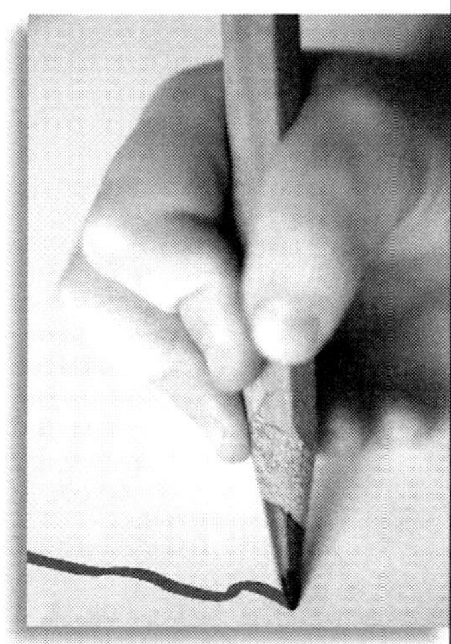

This is a story about a young Swiss girl. As the story unfolds, sketch or draw what comes to mind. Use an 8½ x 11 inch piece of paper and begin at the left-hand edge of the paper.

Heidi lives in the Swiss Alps. One morning, she decides to go for a hike. Her dog, Wolf Wolf, tags along with her. At first, they follow a winding path in the foothills through a field of colorful spring flowers. Soon, they cross over a fast-flowing stream. The sun is warm on Heidi's face and arms. Wolf Wolf wags his tail as they begin to climb upward through the trees. The climb is becoming more steep. A very large mountain looms ahead. Suddenly, there appears on the path in front of them a mountain goat. As they continue to climb, several large birds fly overhead. Two big boulders challenge their climbing skills. A curious Swiss cow with a gonging cow bell observes their progress. After awhile, they come upon a small hut on the side of the mountain. Heidi is beginning to feel hungry and tired so she takes out their lunch. They eat until their stomachs are pleasantly full. The sun is very warm. A tired young girl and her dog curl up and take a nap.

Floor Plan of Your Childhood Home

Mental Fitness Card 65

Draw a floor plan of the home (or one of the homes) where you lived as a child, indicating the location of the doors and windows. Sketch in the furniture as you remember it.

When the floor plan is finished, write a paragraph about some memorable event that took place in the house.

If you prefer, draw a floor plan of the kitchen that you remember best from your childhood. Then, write a paragraph about something that happened in that kitchen.

Rooms in Your Childhood Home

Thinking Card 57

Either draw or describe a favorite room from a house that you lived in as child.

Be as specific as you like.

What furniture and pictures were in the room? What color were the walls or wallpaper pattern?

Write or talk about memories you have of being in that room.

Finish the Line Drawings

Mental Fitness Card 66

Draw these simple lines on an 8½ x 11 inch piece of paper following the format here. Now, begin to add additional lines to each and make a realistic picture. Continue to add even more lines and see what you can develop. Try doing it more than once, developing even more creative ideas each time.

Cut It Out!

Thinking Card 58

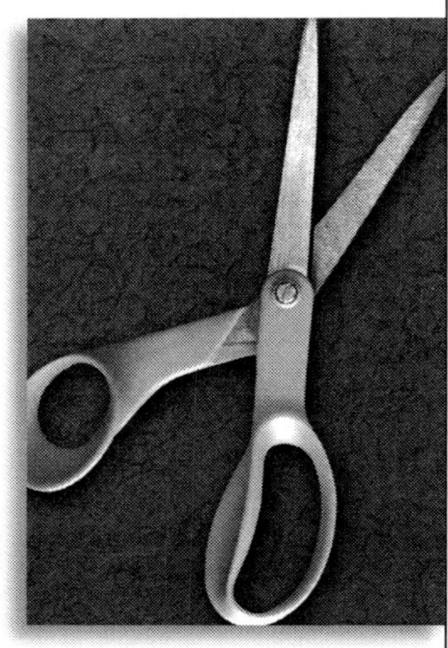

Find a magazine or catalog you plan to discard. Using scissors, cut out photos or pictures of things that interest you.

Try cutting out some figures or objects following along the outline, with all the little twists and turns. You'll be stimulating the coordination between your brain and hand.

After you cut out the pictures, you can make a collage by pasting or taping the pictures to a thick piece of paper or cardboard. Have fun with it, and share your artwork with family and friends!

Tree People

Thinking Card 56

This is a good activity if you like to draw.

If you were a tree, think about what you would look like. Then, do a sketch of how the tree would look. If you think you can't draw, do a very simple sketch. Give the tree a name if you'd like.

Now think of a friend or a family member and draw a tree that would exemplify him or her. You could arrange your trees into a "group picture"— a forest of trees.

Draw What You Hear

Mental Fitness Card 93

Play a recording (tape, CD, old record) of a piece of music that you enjoy. You may want to listen to music on the radio.

While you are listening, draw a picture or pictures of what you hear.

The picture need not be realistic but can simply be lines or shapes or textures or colors that express the ideas or feelings that come to you as you listen.

What to Look for in Works of Art

Mental Fitness Card 82

Find a painting of a well-known artist such as Van Gogh, Picasso or Grant Wood and place it in front of you. (Find pictures in books, magazines, newspapers, local shops where prints are sold, or libraries that loan art prints.)

Now answer these questions:

◆ What kind of lines do you see?

◆ What shapes can you find in the picture?

◆ What colors has the artist used?

◆ Point out the textures such as rough, smooth, soft, hard, prickly, etc.

◆ What mood or feelings do you think the artist was trying to create?

◆ What thoughts come to your mind as you look at this picture?

What to Look for in Works of Art
Thinking Card 66

Find a painting by a well-known artist or just one you really like. (Find pictures in books, magazines, or libraries that loan art prints.) Look at the painting and answer these questions:

◆ What shapes can you find in the picture?

◆ What colors do you see?

◆ How does the picture make you feel?

◆ What thoughts come to mind as you look at the picture?

A Picture Takes the Place of a Word

Mental Fitness Card 90

Write a short letter to a friend using paper and pencil and substituting a picture for a word throughout the letter. Two examples:

I love Wisconsin cheese.

Nobody knows how much I pine for you, dear.

Nursery rhymes lend themselves to this activity. Try "Hi diddle diddle, the cat and the fiddle, the cow jumped over the moon. The little dog laughed to see such a sight and the dish ran away with the spoon."

five

Working Out Mentally with Poetry

Working Out Mentally with Poetry

Goal	To stimulate the brain by using words in the form of poetry.
Cards needed	Mental Fitness Cards 13, 26, 28, 30, 47, 93 Thinking Cards 70, 94
Other resources	Favorite books of poems, variety of music recordings, old newspapers or magazines.
Supplies	Paper, pens/pencils, writing surfaces, overhead projector or bulletin board, tape or CD player, scissors, tape or glue.

Pertinent information

Begin by telling your group: "There is now good evidence that using words in many different ways challenges and stimulates the brain. The feature article, 'Quiet Miracles of the Brain,' in the June 1995 *National Geographic* indicates that four areas of the brain light up when you see, generate, speak and hear words. So poetry—reading, hearing and writing poetry— is excellent brain food."

Daisy Goodwin, editor of *101 Poems That Could Save Your Life: An Anthology of Emotional First Aid* (New York: HarperCollins, 2003), says: "For quick and effective relief for all your emotional ailments without harmful side effects, try a poem—for however bad it is, however low you have sunk, you can be sure that some poet has been there too." The right poem (meaning the one that speaks to you and your situation) at the right time (just when you need it) can put things in perspective and give you a stimulating mental workout.

Also tell your participants: "We tend to embrace life's difficulties so tightly that, at times, it's necessary to give ourselves a break. Like deep breathing, reading poetry can give you a fresh perspective and lift some weight off your shoulders. Even if you've never read poetry before, open any volume and read until you find a piece that speaks to you. Knowing that a poet has chewed on a similar issue, 'spit it out' on paper and repeated the process several times reassures us they know what they're talking about. Rather than using the TV remote to scan through meaningless programs, take up your favorite poetry book and lose yourself."

Listen to poetry

For the group's first session, try choosing some of *your* favorite poems. If you don't have any, ask one of your participants to bring poetry to an informal gathering. Sit in a circle and read a familiar poem aloud—for instance, "The Road Not Taken," by Robert Frost:

> Two roads diverged in a yellow wood,
> And sorry I could not travel both
> And be one traveler, long I stood
> And looked down one as far as I could
> To where it bent in the undergrowth;
>
> Then took the other, as just as fair,
> And having perhaps the better claim,
> Because it was grassy and wanted wear;
> Though as for that, the passing there
> Had worn them really about the same.
>
> And both that morning equally lay
> In leaves no step had trodden black.
> Oh, I kept the first for another day!
> Yet knowing how way leads on to way,
> I doubted if I should ever come back.
>
> I shall be telling this with a sigh
> Somewhere ages and ages hence:
> Two roads diverged in a wood, and I—
> I took the one less traveled by,
> And that has made all the difference.

Ask your participants how this poem speaks to them. If it's difficult for them to put their emotions into words, prompt them: "Do you feel sad or happy after hearing this poem?" Because it speaks to the path we've all chosen to take, feelings of regret may surface for some. For others, it can remind them of decisions they made that benefited them but were unpopular with those around them. Don't let this poem hang in the past. Bring it into the present and ask: "How are we each choosing between paths every day—in our personal choices, but also in the world? There is always more than one way to decide on any given situation. Poetry has a way of expressing this in a more succinct manner."

From here you could open up a discussion about different paths each senior has taken. "What choices have 'made all the difference' in your lives?" Again, try to steer them away from regrets — "If I had done that, life would have been better." Frost's poem can easily stir up regret for not taking a more daring path, but Frost did not intend for his readers to get bogged down in "if only" thinking. Rather, the poem affirms choices made—whether right or wrong, good or bad.

Someone else may have another poem about choosing life paths. I often think of the short poem Richard R. Niebuhr wrote in 1984 called "Pilgrims and Pioneers":

> Pilgrims are persons in motion—passing
> through territories not their own—seeking
> something we might call completion, or per-
> haps the word "clarity" will do as well, a goal to
> which only the spirit's compass points the way.

To encourage comments on this poem, say: "At any age, we are still seeking and choosing. What are you choosing today? What are you seeking? How would you know if you had found completion or clarity in your life?" These and other questions should stimulate a lively discussion.

Daisy Goodwin's book, mentioned earlier, is indexed by emotions. You can flip to the index and look under such categories as "Birthday Blues," "Career Crisis," "First Wrinkle." Under the category "Instant Moral Fiber," you'll find this poem by Nasim Hikmet, translated from the Turkish by Richard McKane:

> ***24th September 1945***
> The best sea: has yet to be crossed.
> The best child: has yet to be born.
> The best days: have yet to be lived;
> And the best word that I wanted to say to you
> Is the word that I have not yet said.

There *are* good things ahead. Suggest your readers choose a poem like this one when they feel there's nothing to look forward to. Especially when your participants are feeling left behind in the rush of life, it is important for them to know that more good times await them. Many of the seniors with whom we work look to the past for their "best days." But a poem like this could challenge them and encourage them to continue looking for that best sea to cross.

◆ Read a poem aloud

Mental Fitness Cards
13, 28

Studies show that when we read aloud or listen to someone reading, we use different parts of the brain than when we read silently. Reading poetry aloud not only gives the brain a workout, it also allows you and others to hear the poem in a new way. Read some poems that speak to you and show the group how delightful it is to hear poetry read. One of my favorite poems, by David Whyte (Washington: Many Rivers Press, 2002), speaks to everyone who struggles to feel fulfilled. Have one of your participants read this poem aloud, or read it yourself:

Enough

Enough. These few words are enough.

If not these words, this breath.
If not this breath, this sitting here.

This opening to the life
we have refused
again and again,
until now.

Until now.

I have used this poem as a teaching tool to remind people that we're already enough "as is." Wherever we are in life is enough, and what we're doing right now is enough. Ask your group, "What do you hear in this poem?" Ask the participants to express their feelings. "How does the poem speak to you personally? Does the poem make you feel sad and lonely or nurtured and validated? What do you think the poet was feeling when he wrote this?"

Next, ask your group about the poem's subject: "Are you enough right now? If you don't feel enough right now, when have you felt like you were enough?" (You may want to refer to Mental Fitness Card 28, "Try to Remember," and have your group read Nelson Mandela's words as a reminder of their self-worth, underlining the important words in the speech.)

◆ Memorize a poem

Reassure your group that anyone can memorize a poem: "Many people think you lose your ability to memorize when you get older. The truth is that we just need to exercise the skill to keep it going strong." Request that someone recite poems they learned in grade school or *Psalms* they memorized in Sunday school. Ask your group to remember how they memorized the alphabet—using the ABC song (Mental Fitness Card 30). (Usually everyone starts singing, which is great!) "Many of us remember our ABCs because of that catchy tune," you point out. "While the letters are processed on the left side of the brain, the rhythm and music tend to be processed on the right. When you put the two together, it reinforces memory. My mother taught me the books of the *New Testament* 30 years ago by setting them to a tune; I can still sing all the books."

My brother enjoyed Wendy Cope's poem "The Orange" (from *Good Poems* by Garrison Keillor, New York: Viking, 2002) so much that he set it to music and thus memorized the poem. Ask the members of your group to see what they can do with Cope's poem:

At lunchtime I bought a huge orange—
The size of it made us all laugh.
I peeled it and shared it with Robert and Dave—
They got quarters and I had a half.

And that orange, it made me so happy,
As ordinary things often do
Just lately. The shopping. A walk in the park.
This is peace and contentment. It's new.

The rest of the day was quite easy.
I did all the jobs on my list
And enjoyed them and had some time over.
I love you. I'm glad I exist.

Ask your participants to memorize this poem or a Bible verse or a key sentence from Nelson Mandela's speech. They can set it to music if that helps. Tell them not to get discouraged. "Expect that it will take longer to memorize than you think," tell them, "but rest assured that the more you work on this skill, the sharper your abilities become."

COGNITIVE ADAPTATION

Use Thinking Card 70 ("Rhymes and Riddles"). Sometimes we don't realize we've already memorized a poem or have the ability to do so. If your participants have a greater cognitive impairment or need more encouragement, ask them, "Did your parents or grandparents tell you rhymes and riddles when you were a child? My friend Sarah remembers her mother often reciting: 'Patience is a virtue/Virtue is a grace/Grace was a little girl who never washed her face.' She also quoted Robert Louis Stevenson: 'The world is so full of a number of things/I'm sure we should all be as happy as kings.'"

Then ask the group, "Did you ever sing rhymes while jumping rope?" As you ask questions, give time and encouragement for the participants to share. You could also make this an intergenerational event by having grandchildren or young school children in to share poems or songs they have memorized.

Nelson Mandela's speech (Mental Fitness Card 28) is well worth memorizing. It starts with two intriguing sentences:

Our deepest fear is not that we are inadequate.
Our deepest fear is that we are powerful beyond measure.

Tell your group, "Repeat, repeat and repeat these two lines. Repeat them in front of a mirror. Repeat them while you're getting dressed. Repeat them to a friend. Work on memorizing for several minutes; then leave it and return to it another time. Gradually it will come." Then add the next pairing of sentences (but always starting with the first two):

Our deepest fear is not that we are inadequate.
Our deepest fear is that we are powerful beyond measure.
It is our light, not our darkness, that most frightens us.
We ask ourselves, who am I to be brilliant, gorgeous, talented and fabulous?

(continued)

Write a poem

Mental Fitness Card 26

Let your participants know that what they bring to a blank page is enough—one's experience in life, what one has—*enough* to provide an excellent starting place to write a poem.

Before beginning, a good activity is to have folks put new endings on familiar poems: "Roses are red, Violets are blue . . ." (Mental Fitness Card 26). The new endings need not make sense and may even be ridiculous and outlandish. One woman in her eighties wrote: "Roses are red, Violets are blue. Your feet stink, And so do you."

Encourage creativity and brainstorming as you gather new endings to old favorites like "'Twas the Night Before Christmas" and "Hickory, Dickory Dock." When you have a few poems reworked, post them on a bulletin board so others can enjoy these new twists to old gems.

Kenneth Koch wrote a book in the late 1970s entitled *I Never Told Anybody: Teaching Poetry Writing in a Nursing Home* (New York: Vintage Books, 1978). While he addresses the frail elderly, many of his thoughts and methods can be used in teaching adults of any activity level or age. His book, which contains many poems written by older adults, should give your group ideas and, possibly, subjects for new poems. Suggest a poem "about the quietest moment you've ever experienced. Use the word 'quiet' in the poem. Here's an example by Fred Richardson:

> I always was quiet
> And my mother always had to send my
> Sisters into the room
> To see what made me so quiet.

When the poem's read aloud, the word *quiet* is spoken quietly."

Make sure to tell the group, "Rhyme isn't necessary in good poetry. Just explain how you're feeling. Read other poetry to gain inspiration."

I highly recommend Koch's book because he makes writing poetry seem like something people any age could handle easily and enjoy. He also realizes some older participants have physical limits affecting their writing—poor eyesight, shaking hands and so on—and he suggests the facilitator or another participant act as a scribe. Kenneth Koch also suggests writing a sentence or two about a simple idea—color, for instance. His student Mary Tkalec put the name of a color in every line:

I like green; I used to see so many greens on the farm.
I used to wear green, and sometimes my mother
    couldn't find me
Because I was green in the green.

As Koch's students responded creatively, he took greater risks, asking them to imagine themselves as an ocean. In response, Harry Siegel wrote this:

I, the ocean, on stormy days am always wrecking things
And when I'm quiet and not stormy
I'm singing along with the people on the houseboats
And enjoying the young people swimming in me
Letting the folks fish in me.

Don't forget to recognize the hard work of your students. Display their poems or set up a poetry reading group, inviting staff, family and loved ones. It's a wonderful celebration of their success and creativity.

Writing list poems

Ask your participants to write a list poem—a simple listing of ideas focused on a particular subject—while they are seated around a table (Mental Fitness Card 47). Marge Engelman provides these examples from one of her classes:

1. List the good things about being over 60.

2. List the good things you received from your mother or grandmother or father or grandfather.

3. List things that you love to do.

4. List things that you want to do.

Taking off on the theme of good things about being over 60, Marge writes:

I like being over 60 because I can
Sleep as late as I like in the morning.
Plan my day's schedule with no worry of others' needs.
Share my life stories and people will appreciate them,
Most of the time.
Go without my bra and nobody will notice—or care.
Sing as loud as I like in the shower and no one will hear me.
Stop buying coloring for my hair and just enjoy letting it go gray.

Writing acrostic poems

You can make writing list poems more challenging by introducing the concept of acrostic poems, in which you use the letters of a chosen word, such as Christmas, Thanksgiving or a word of the group's choosing. Encourage the group to stick with the theme of the word. Here's an example:

Mental Fitness Card 47

Summer

Summer heat wraps around us.
Urchins play ball in the alleys.
Mosquitoes sneak around and bite.
Mornings may be misty and musty.
Evenings are punctuated with fireflies.
Rain washes the world within an inch of its life.

COGNITIVE ADAPTATION

Use Thinking Card 94 ("Accidental Poems"). If your participants are having a hard time coming up with lines, ask them to use headlines from old newspapers or magazines. To set up this activity, gather materials and possibly pick one or two participants to help you cut out headlines. Gather the participants in a small group and have them put the headlines together to create poetry. Don't worry about the poems rhyming or making total sense. The goal of the activity is to get the participants to put thoughts together to create a poem. You may also need to cut out or create other words that are useful as transitions between your headlines. Paste the lines on a sheet of paper and encourage your participants to read their works aloud.

Draw what you hear

Another way to encourage poetry writing is to listen to music that helps draw out feelings. Begin by playing a piece of classical music or a melody without words. Feel free to play music your group is not used to. I often play music they're unaccustomed to hearing in order to encourage being in the present rather than only reminiscing. I have had groups of older adults listen to anything from Alanis Morissette to the St. Olaf Choir.

Begin playing the music, then prompt your group by asking: "How does the music make you feel?" Encourage everyone to write down feeling words, emotional memories and dramatic encounters. Recently I picked up my niece for coffee. As soon as she got into the car, she turned the radio to a hard rock station, one I don't like much. When we got to the coffee shop, I asked, "What's going on? How did that music make you feel? Tell me why you chose that music." Instead of turning off her music, I wanted to tune into her and ask about the music and what it meant to her.

Ask: "What rhythm do you hear? How does that make you feel?" If you're listening to a song with words, ask them how the words make them feel. "What words do you think of as you're listening to the music? Do you see any scenes or specific places or people? Do you see any colors? Think of anybody or any place?" Suggest that your poets close their eyes and, "When you open your eyes, begin to write thoughts down, even if they feel scattered."

Thinking Card 94

Mental Fitness Card 93

You could play music as the group is coming in before the session begins. Choose your own poem and pick out a piece of music that speaks to you. Share this with your group. You could also have a participant choose the music and encourage the others to write about it. Kenneth Koch suggests you play Mozart's Symphonia no. 40. Then read from a poem that shows how poetry talks about music, as in these lines by Shakespeare:

> Orpheus with his lute made trees,
> And the mountain tops that freeze,
> Bow themselves when he did sing . . .

Walt Whitman writes about the ordinary sounds that are a kind of music in his poem *Song of Myself.*

> I hear the bravuras of birds, bustle of growing wheat, gossip of flames,
>   clack of sticks cooking my meals . . .
> The ring of alarm bells, the cry of fire, the whirr of swift-streaking
>   engines and horse-carts with premonitory tinkles and colored lights.
> The steam whistle . . .

Marge Engelman suggests that participants draw a picture of what they hear (Mental Fitness Card 93). It can be something as abstract as shapes. Then turn these pictures into poems.

Play Aaron Copeland's "Our Town" and encourage your group to relax enough to listen and write. There is a distinct theme running through Copeland's piece. Ask your group: "What words come to mind when you hear this music?" Give them time and encourage them to write down words, in no particular order. Then ask, "What mood does this music describe to you?" Again, have them write down words randomly.

Using Whitman's poem, above, start your own poem with "I hear . . ." and tell your group to fill in the words you put on the page. Reiterate that the poem need not rhyme. Also remind your group that whatever they bring to the session and is certainly good enough. They aren't going to be graded!

Writing Haiku

My poet brother uses haiku when he teaches others to write poetry. Haiku (HY-koo) is a traditional Japanese verse form notable for being compact and suggestive. In three lines, totaling seventeen syllables and measuring five-seven-five syllables, a great haiku presents a web of linked ideas requiring the listener to hear with an active mind.

This form was developed by the Japanese poet Basho (1644–94). Traditionally, a haiku presents a pair of contrasting images. One suggests a time and a place; the other image is of something vivid that won't last long. Working together, the images bring out moods and emotions. The poet does not comment; he or she lets the reader make the connection. Here's a haiku by Basho:

> Now the swinging bridge
> Is quieted with creepers
> Like our tendrilled life

Basho also writes:

> How reluctantly
> the bee emerges from deep
> within the peony

Ask the participants: "Is he talking only about bees or is he really talking about human emotions? He could be representing both. Is the bee actually inside a peony, or does this haiku talk about the poet deep within a thought?" Discuss with your group what they feel when they hear such a poem. Every response is valid.

Homework

Challenge the participants to write their own haiku. Tell them: "Don't get hung up on creating exactly seventeen syllables. Try to capture a broad feeling while staying in the neighborhood of seventeen syllables and three lines. The point is to write and then share your haiku." It can be a wonderful experience.

five
Participant Materials

Read Aloud

Mental Fitness Card 13

Studies show that when we read aloud or listen to someone reading, we use different parts of the brain than when we read silently.

Most of us read to ourselves in silence, and that stimulates one part of the brain. Reading is an important mental exercise.

To do something different, read aloud to yourself for awhile.

Then, try reading aloud to someone else.

You might try alternating the roles of reader and listener. It will take longer than reading in silence, but it will activate different parts of the brain.

Try to Remember

Mental Fitness Card 28

"Our deepest fear is not that we are inadequate. Our deepest fear is that we are powerful beyond measure. It is our light, not our darkness, that most frightens us. We ask ourselves, who am I to be brilliant, gorgeous, talented and fabulous? Actually, who are you not to be? You are a child of God. Your playing small doesn't serve the world . . . As we let our light shine, we unconsciously give other people permission to do the same . . ." Adapted from a speech by Nelson Mandela.

Underline the important words in this speech. Write a headline that portrays the meaning of the words. Decide on a tune and sing the words to it. Read them aloud. Now put aside the words and write as much as you can remember. Did you surprise yourself at how well you did?

Memory and Music

Mental Fitness Card 30

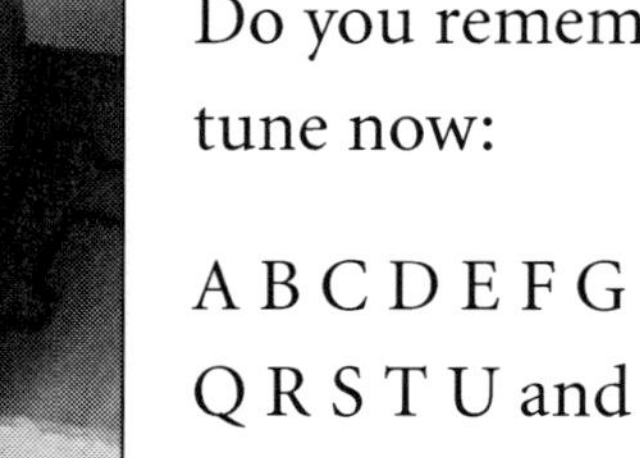

Do you remember how you learned your ABCs? Sing the tune now:

A B C D E F G . . . H I J K L M N O P . . .
Q R S T U and V . . . W X and Y and Z.
Now I know my ABCs, tell me what you think of me.

Why do you think you remember this so well over so many years? It is probably because the letters are processed in the left brain and the rhythm and music tend to be processed in the right brain. When you put the two together, it reinforces memory.

Try this activity: Make a list of 4–6 errands you need to do in the next several days. (It could be letters to write, cards to send or phone calls to make.) Now, pick a tune that you like and set the list to music. You'll be surprised how your memory is enhanced.

Rhymes and Riddles

Thinking Card 70

Did your parents or grandparents tell you rhymes and riddles when you were a child?

Did you ever sing rhymes while jumping rope?

Can you still recite some of those rhymes? Try it and see.

Introduce these rhymes to your children or grandchildren and enjoy them together.

New Ending for Old Beginnings

Mental Fitness Card 26

"Roses are red, Violets are blue . . ."

Write a new ending for this familiar Valentine verse. Be innovative, such as one person in her 80s who wrote:

"Roses are red, Violets are blue. Your feet stink and so do you."

Try a number of different endings.

Another familiar verse that lends itself to new endings is: "Thirty days have September, April, June and November." You may have heard the nonsensical ending: "Thirty days have September, April, June and no wonder, all the rest have peanut butter, except Grandmother and she rides a little red tricycle."

No new ending is too ridiculous. Use the first lines of other poems that you know such as "The golden rod is yellow" or "'Twas the night before Christmas."

Things I'm Not Going to Do Now That I'm Over 60

Mental Fitness Card 47

As we get older, we sometimes think, "Well, I'm not going to do that any more," or "I've done that for the last time."

Do some brainstorming around this statement: "Things I'm not going to do now that I'm over 60 (or 70 or 80 or 90)." You have permission to be outrageous. Stretch your imagination. Think of the things you're tired of doing. To prime the pump, here are several ideas generated by some over-70 people:

- I'm not going to get out of bed early in the morning at 6:00 a.m.

- I'm not going to be so concerned with what others think.

- I'm not going to go somewhere if I don't want to.

- I'm not going to restrain myself from spitting.

Accidental Poems

Thinking Card 94

Take a stack of old newspapers that you're going to discard and cut headlines out of them.

Then, try to arrange these lines into a poem. If you're having trouble making sense out of your line fragments, go back to the newspaper to cut out other words that are useful as transitions between your headlines. Paste the lines on a sheet of paper and appreciate your literary talent!

This can also be done in pairs or in small groups.

Draw What You Hear

Mental Fitness Card 93

Play a recording (tape, CD, old record) of a piece of music you enjoy. You may want to listen to music on the radio.

While you are listening, draw a picture or pictures of what you hear.

The picture need not be realistic but can simply be lines or shapes or textures or colors that express the ideas or feelings that come to you as you listen.

six

Stimulating Imagination through Discussion

Stimulating Imagination through Discussion

Goal	To encourage your participants to stretch their imaginations and to stimulate new and creative ideas.
Cards needed	Mental Fitness Cards 46, 48, 50, 51, 53, 55 Thinking Cards 31, 34, 52
Supplies	Paper, pens/pencils, writing surface, overhead projector or bulletin board.

COGNITIVE ADAPTATION

Remember that leading a discussion group with people who have some dementia means that you as the leader need to be accommodating. The discussion may not always follow a thread or make sense. Be very flexible.

My experience

Some of the best times I've shared with older adults have been in discussion groups. I started a group when I opened an independent-living apartment building in Wisconsin. Every morning, a bunch of folks, mostly women, would gather for coffee. I asked them if they would like to have an official discussion group, to which they replied, "We already talk about things." I said, "No, you have organ recitals—you know, when you start comparing who has had which organ taken out." They laughed.

It took some convincing, but they agreed to let me "experiment" with them. I started by presenting a topic and leading the discussion, but I really had to pull ideas out of them. Initially it was a lot of work. But, after we had held several sessions, the group really started getting into it—sharing opinions, thoughts and feelings. They even came up with their own topics, after a fashion. Besides being a mentally stimulating activity, I witnessed this group of women come alive. Their interests in everyday life heightened. They were hungry to learn more, to imagine more, to get together more often. This whole discussion idea, which they thought was silly at first, turned into a time to be treasured. So be patient with your group and allow the discussions to blossom.

Pertinent information

You might tell the participants, "Remember, even if it doesn't go well the first time, keep at it." In the beginning, choose topics the group has some knowledge about. After they're used to the idea of discussion groups, move into a wider range of topics. Remember, our focus in this session is to stimulate the imagination. Review of discussion rules is always a good way to begin a session.

Discussion ground rules revisited

Discussion groups are a great way for older adults to state opinions, argue, learn, stretch mentally and join in. Along with basic rules for discussion, I also include information on listening skills:

1. Have an uninterrupted space, such as a quiet room where you can close the door. (I also inform aides, managers and nurses that I'm having a closed-door activity.)

2. Put the chairs in a circle; circles create a sense of equality.

3. Set ground rules (or guidelines, if you like that word better) with the group—
   - Everyone gets a chance to speak, if they wish.
   - No judging.
   - Everyone is entitled to their opinion.
   - Questions are good.
   - The facilitator doesn't have all the answers.

4. Then review good listening skills—
   - Listen with your eyes as well as your ears.
   - Ask who, what, where, when and why questions.
   - Paraphrasing what someone else has said lets them know you heard them.

Warm-up discussion

The list of discussion possibilities is endless. Some participants may find certain topics ridiculous but with your encouragement their reservations will vanish. Here are some ideas (use no more than one or two of these topics in a session):

1. If someone gave you a barrel of pickles, what would you do?

2. What would you do if someone gave you an Arabian horse?

3. If someone gave you a million dollars, how would you spend it?

4. If you were free to do whatever you wanted, what would it be?

5. If you were stranded on a desert island, who would you want to be with?

6. What would you like to clean, fix up or paint if you could?

7. What's an ideal vacation?

8. Who or what would you like to be if you were reincarnated?

9. If you could create something beautiful for the world, what would it be?

10. If you made a movie, what would its plot be?

11. What would you like to invent? What would it do?

12. If you could choose a different name, what would it be? Why?

13. What do you think of when you look at the moon?

14. If you could invite a famous person to come to your group, who would you invite?

What if?

Mental Fitness Card 48

Today everyone is invited to think crazy, zany thoughts. Be freewheeling, even playful, as you explore some of the weirdest topics you and your group can think of (Mental Fitness Card 48).

If you were . . .

Mental Fitness Card 55

If your group is big, I suggest having participants answer these questions on their own and bring their answers to the session. If the group is small and there are participants who depend on others, have them team up (Mental Fitness Card 55).

COGNITIVE ADAPTATION

Thinking Card 52 ("If You Were . . .") has pretty much the same information as Mental Fitness Card 55. You'll need to play a less (or more) intrusive role in the discussion, depending on your group's level of cognitive ability.

Thinking Card 52

Breathing break and stretch break

Now that the creative juices are flowing, it's time to stretch and breathe. Tell your participants: "Either standing or sitting, reach your arms up to the ceiling, moving them to the side. Then shrug your shoulders like you're hugging your ears, and release." Repeat this. Remind the group to take in a good, deep breath on the count of four, hold it for seven and let it go over a count of eight.

Solving real life problems

Mental Fitness Card 46

This can be great fun, even if you're solving things that are sometimes very frustrating in everyday life. Encourage your group to let loose. Mental Fitness Card 46 has great suggestions, so put it on an overhead or give each participant a copy.

A time box

Mental Fitness Card 50

If your group is big, break into smaller groups so people work as teams. Tell your teams: "Decide what story you, as a group, would like to tell distant generations about the world as it is today. Or think together about what you'd put in a time capsule."

Thinking Card 31

COGNITIVE ADAPTATION

Thinking Card 31 ("A Time Box") provides easy-to-follow directions. I suggest conducting this activity as a group session, asking participants to share their thoughts. You could write suggestions on a flip chart or overhead projector.

Completing sentences

Ask participants to fill out the following incomplete sentences. Encourage participants to work on these questions on their own:

1. People think of me as . . .

2. I miss . . .

3. The thing I like best about myself is . . . (This one can be difficult, as people in this generation were taught not to brag about themselves. And people from certain cultural backgrounds feel obligated to be modest. If participants are struggling, ask them to write down positive things others have said about them.)

4. I would like to see . . .

5. It is fun to . . .

6. Five years from now I . . . (Sometimes asking older adults to speculate five years in the future brings on comments such as, "I'll probably be dead." If that happens, inform them that they should consider themselves still living.)

If group members are willing, share what they have written and discuss their ideas.

COGNITIVE ADAPTATION

Thinking Card 34 ("I've Learned That . . . ") gets at what we've learned from life and what's important to us. Read some of the quotations and ask, in a large group, whether anyone has similarly important life lessons they would like to pass along.

Homework

End the session on a light note, asking participants to imagine they are party planners. Follow the suggestions on Mental Fitness Card 51 ("Parties for Older Adults"). If you still have time left over at the end of the session, start this activity, but then send them off to finish the project on their own.

What If

Mental Fitness Card 48

We are usually very proper people and think very rational thoughts. But today, you are given permission to think crazy, zany thoughts. Be free-wheeling and flippant. Write six answers to each of these questions.

- ◆ What if we had no cars?

- ◆ What if clouds had strings attached which hung down to the earth?

- ◆ If the moon could talk, what would it say?

- ◆ What if we lived to be 200 years old?

- ◆ What if we never had to sleep?

- ◆ What would happen in the world if water did not freeze?

- ◆ What if the earth were shrouded in fog and all you could see of people was their feet?

By now, you have probably thought of some of your own "What if's?" Have fun!

If You Were . . .

Mental Fitness Card 55

Answer each of these questions, preferably in writing, explaining why for each one.

- If you were an animal, what animal would you be?

- If you were a color, what color would you be?

- If you were a musical instrument, which would you be?

- If you were a flower, which kind would you be?

- If you were able to live anywhere in the world, where would you live?

- If you were a holiday, which one would you be?

- If you were an article of clothing, what would you be?

- If you were a kind of candy, which kind would you be?

- If you wrote a book, what would the title be?

Now, review your answers and decide on at least three adjectives that describe the kind of person you are.

If You Were . . .

Thinking Card 52

Answer each of these questions, either in writing or out loud. Explain why for each one.

- If you were an animal, what animal would you be?

- If you were a color, what color would you be?

- If you were a musical instrument, which would you be?

- If you were a flower, which kind would you be?

- If you were able to live anywhere in the world, where would you live?

- If you were a holiday, which one would you be?

- If you were an article of clothing, what would you be?

- If you were a kind of candy, which kind would you be?

- If you wrote a book, what would the title be?

Brainstorming—Solving Real Life Problems

Mental Fitness Card 46

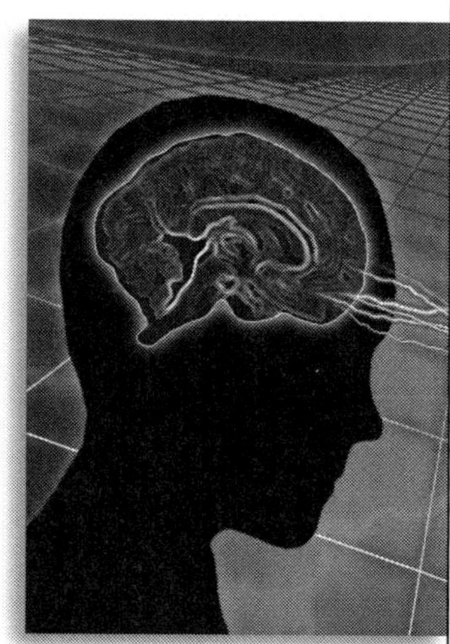

Brainstorming is a wonderful way to help solve real life problems. Often, we think of only a couple ideas to solve a problem. Brainstorming presses us to come up with many possible solutions. Pick one or two of the following and brainstorm to your heart's content.

◆ What can you do when time after time the doctor keeps you waiting?

◆ What can you do to stop worrying?

◆ Your children give you a gift that you can't use and yet you don't want to offend them. What do you do?

◆ We tend to celebrate 50th wedding anniversaries by having an open house or a dinner party for the family and friends. What other ways could we celebrate?

◆ What can you do when you feel lonely?

Now, think of a problem that you have and brainstorm it.

A Time Box

Mental Fitness Card 50

What things would you leave in a time box that would tell future civilizations what life was like at this time?

Think of at least 12 items that you would include.

Now make a list of what you would have put in a time box 50 years ago.

Again, think of at least 12 items.

A time box is often included in the cornerstone of a building. Think of at least 5 other places to put a time box where it would be safe.

A Time Box

Thinking Card 31

What things would you leave in a time box to tell future civilizations what life was like at this time?

Why do you think each item should be included?

Are these items different from what you would have put in the box 50 years ago?

Completing Sentences

1. People think of me as . . .

2. I miss . . .

3. The thing I like best about myself is . . .

4. I would like to see . . .

5. It is fun to . . .

6. Five years from now I . . .

I've Learned That . . .

Thinking Card 34

H. Jackson Brown Jr. wrote a book entitled *Live and Learn and Pass It On: People Ages 5 to 95 Share What They've Discovered About Life, Love and Other Good Stuff.* Some quotes from his book:

- I've learned that when your husband cooks, you should compliment everything he fixes.   —*Age 77*

- I've learned that even when I have pains, I don't have to be a pain.   —*Age 82*

- I've learned that you can tell a lot about a man by the way he handles three things: a rainy holiday, lost luggage and tangled Christmas tree lights.   —*Age 52*

- I've learned that I don't feel my age as long as I focus on my dreams instead of my regrets.   —*Age 83*

What have you learned that you would like to pass along?

Parties for Adults

Mental Fitness Card 51

Imagine that you have started a service that plans and organizes parties for older adults. Suggest four possible themes for parties that people over 60 would enjoy.

For each party idea, plan invitations, decorations, favors and food to follow the theme. Do not be concerned about money.

Be as creative as you possibly can. Let wild ideas run rampant. Try for new and different ideas.

Is there a way you might actually carry out some of your party ideas?

seven

Sharpening All Five Senses

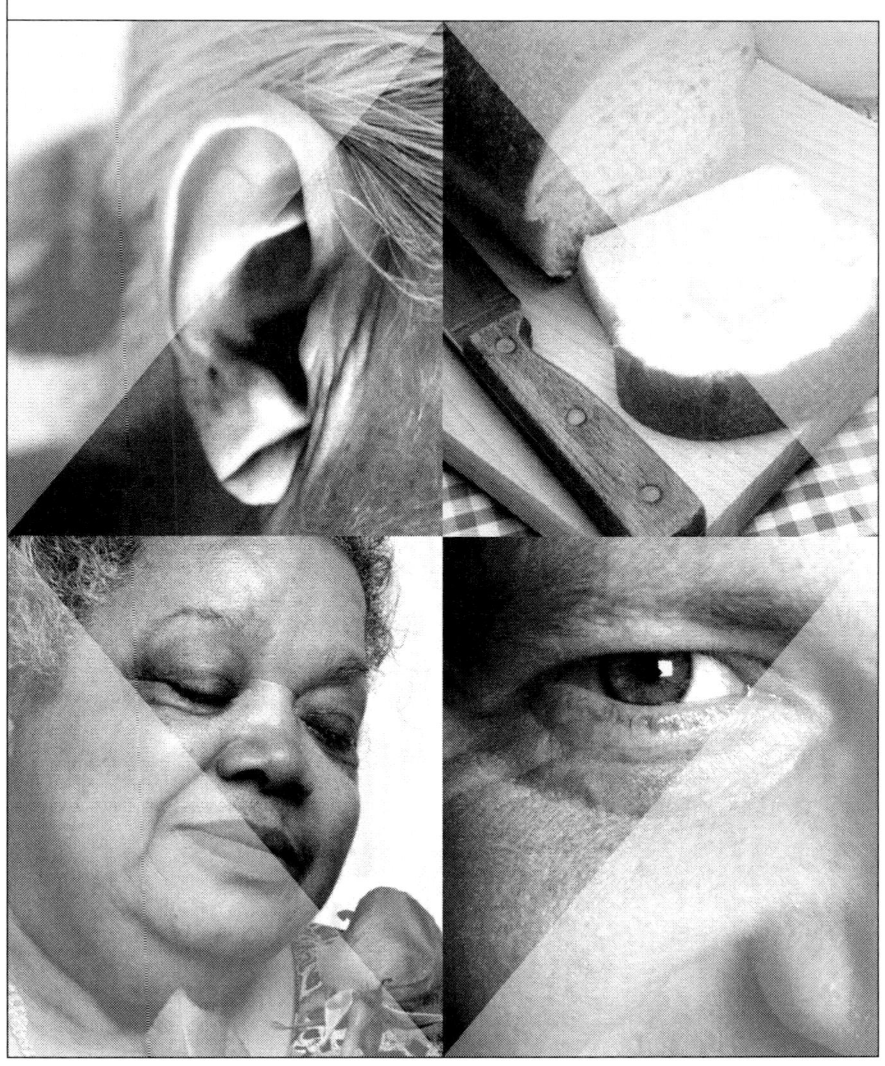

seven

Sharpening All Five Senses

Goal

To increase the power of the senses—to wake up parts of the brain and increase awareness of the present.

Cards needed

Mental Fitness Cards 1, 83, 84, 91, 97, 99, 100
Thinking Cards 67, 68, 71, 72, 99

Supplies

Coffee/tea, paper, pens/pencils, writing surfaces, overhead projector or bulletin board.

Pertinent information

This session is divided into four sections: seeing, hearing, smelling and tasting, and touching. Ask the participants, "How many of you take your five senses for granted?" Tell them, "In today's session, we're going to focus on waking up all five senses. In doing so, we'll be using different parts of the brain, thus exercising our brains. There are so many treasures to experience—to see, hear, taste, smell and touch. This is a session that challenges each of us to pay attention to things we don't ordinarily attend to."

I realize some participants have a sensory deficit. That's okay; they can still get a lot out of the session. Acknowledge their loss and let them express their frustration or sadness at not having that sense.

You can explain: "Our senses seem to be dulled by years of living. Sometimes we say, 'I've seen it all' or 'I've heard it all.' (I hope you resist saying that!). But have we? Or do we need to sharpen our senses to see the sunset anew, listen to the birds again, savor our soup, sniff the lilacs and enjoy the feel of a kitten's fur? Making conscious efforts to be more aware can bring a great deal of joy into our lives."

Tell the group: "I'm going to remind you that we take our five senses for granted. Then I'm going to help you increase your senses' power. We will need to pay attention, focus and practice. Although this may seem easy to do, tuning into something we generally do automatically (like breathing) takes a conscious effort." You may also need to remind the group about opening their "new brains." If you experience new sensations, too, let them know. Older adults respect facilitators who are also learners.

Warm up—breathing

Start off this session by having everyone get comfortable sitting, standing or even lying on the floor. Ask them, "How many of you have been practicing your breathing?" Give positive support and then review the 4-7-8 pattern; have them go through the sequence four times.

Seeing

Vision is by far our most important sensory channel. Some researchers say that approximately 90 percent of the information our brains receive comes through the eyes. We're always looking, but what do we actually see?

You may have a number of participants who struggle with vision, whether it's basic changes that happen to all of us or specialized problems, such as macular degeneration or cataracts. Briefly explain to your group eyesight changes throughout the lifespan:

◆ Difficulty focusing close up, which begins in the 40s

◆ Increased susceptibility to glare, greater difficulty seeing at dusk and more trouble detecting moving objects—these begin in our 50s

◆ Decreasing ability to distinguish fine details, beginning in our 70s

Observing it all—really seeing

Ask participants to look around the room. Ask them to list every object they see, from the largest item to the smallest detail. Give this activity plenty of time. Encourage participants not just to look, but to *really see.* Most people are amazed at the long list they generate and will admit that many items on their list usually go unnoticed. Share the lists, compare and talk about things you don't usually take in.

Encourage participants to sit at different places at the table (this is also good for breaking ruts). I always suggest, "Sit at a different place tonight and see what you notice." We did this at our house one evening. (We have a combined household—my dad, his wife, my husband and me.) When I set our specific napkin holders at different spots, my dad said, "Hey, this isn't my spot." To which I replied, "It is tonight." All of us commented that we saw things differently from our new perspective. We became more observant that evening; our visual awareness was heightened. Try it!

COGNITIVE ADAPTATION

The directions on Thinking Card 67 ("Really Seeing") provide good guidelines for the facilitator. The key with cognitive impairments is for you, the facilitator, to be energized and to ask questions that guide the group. If participants can't name things, help them with "word find." Give lots of praise along the way.

What is in your hand?

This is a wonderful way to enhance noticing skills. Tell your group, "Observe without judgment." Too often when we are asked to concentrate on a part of us—in this case, our hands—we focus on what's wrong with them. American society doesn't seem to value the wrinkles in older hands. As a grade school child, I used to play games where we were instructed to hold out our hands. When I did and others looked at them, some exclaimed, "You've got wrinkles in your hand. You've got granny hands." I was hurt from that teasing and chose to hide my hands from then on. Fortunately today, I don't hide my hands. They are good hands. With many wrinkles and lots of dry skin, they're still *my* hands. Say to your group, "Instead of focusing on how many wrinkles you have or how your hands used to look, observe them as if you had never seen a hand before."

The card also suggests getting a book on palm reading (or inviting someone in to talk with your group about palm reading). I realize this is a touchy subject in some facilities and with some groups. You need to do what's best for your group. If you do go in for the palm reading, follow the directions on the card. And if you trace hands, write the observations from the reading within the hand tracing. Find a place to display the hands.

COGNITIVE ADAPTATION

The directions on Thinking Card 68 ("What's in Your Hand?") help you walk the group through observation of their hands. I suggest they also trace their hands. Depending on their cognitive abilities, participants can either write words of description or color the hands.

Hearing

In the 21st century we are constantly bombarded with sounds and noises from radio, television, cars, airplanes, cash registers and crowded rooms. It's hard to hear single sounds; rarely do we enjoy silence. Often, in self-defense, we tune out. If our hearing is not quite as good as it used to be, we find the accumulation of sounds disturbing. (You may want to pause and talk about hearing loss at this point. Remind the group that, as we age, we tend to have increasing difficulty hearing higher frequencies. This affects more men than women.) With these next activities we will strive to recover sensitivity to individual sounds and develop a new appreciation for those sounds. We also need to focus our attention on being present, sitting quietly and listening.

The sounds around us

Ask participants to be very quiet and observe the sounds they hear. Encourage them to close their eyes so they can focus on hearing. While their eyes are closed, ask the following questions: "Is the heating system humming? Is there a dog barking? Is the wind blowing? Are windows rattling? Are people talking in another room? Is a television playing?" After about three minutes, ask participants to write down what they heard and then share their observations with a neighbor.

Sharpen your hearing

This is a wonderful activity for improving hearing and concentration. Some may find this exercising frustrating at first; the room needs to be very quiet for this to work well. Follow the suggestions on the card and if you see some participants giving up, encourage them to close their eyes and really listen. You may want to say: "Sometimes we tune out right away because 'our hearing is bad.' Today, try to focus on what you *can* hear, rather than what you can't. Sit still and be silent and just listen."

Soothing sounds, irritating sounds

Ask the participants to list the 10 sounds that are most soothing to them. Next ask them for the 10 most irritating sounds. You can play samples of sounds on a tape recorder, then ask participants to write down a word or a sentence about each sound. Make a tape recording of sounds like:

1. A clock ticking
2. Toilet flushing
3. Pans banging
4. Door slamming
5. Chair or door creaking
6. Doorbell ringing
7. Ice cubes going into a glass
8. Television blaring
9. Kids laughing
10. More!

Mental Fitness Card 91

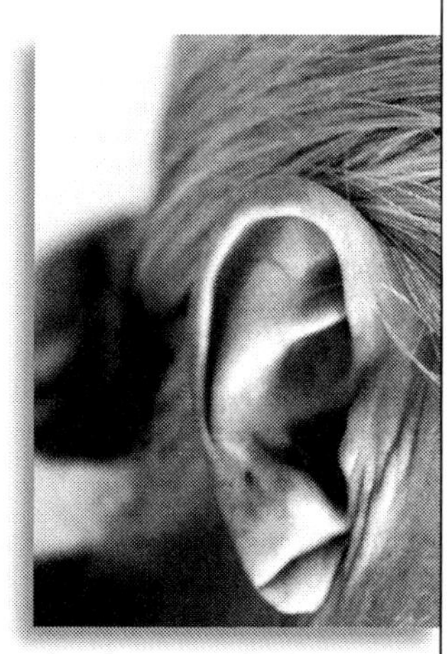

Thinking Card 99

Use the same sounds on the tape recording, but ask the participants—as a group—what they think each sound is and how it makes them feel. Remember, it doesn't matter if they put the correct name to the sound. I would also suggest you use Thinking Card 99 ("Music and Mood"). Music certainly affects our moods. It lets people with almost any cognitive impairment express themselves. Try using music to bring "sundowners" (those who become agitated as night approaches) from one mood to another. Follow the directions on the card. Start with slow, sad music; then move to peppy music. This Thinking Card is a good one to use as dementia progresses. Remember, enjoyment of music is one of the last activities to disappear.

Smelling and tasting

A recent survey on smell done by *National Geographic* magazine indicates that "aging does not bring a uniform decline in 'smellability.'" Ask your group: "Do you think our sense of smell actually declines? Or is it just that we fail to pay enough attention to scents and if we train ourselves it might improve our sense of smell?" Recognizing that no feelings are incorrect, let them share their thoughts.

Smell and taste are closely related, as some of the following activities show. Ask the group, "What happens to your sense of taste when your nose is stuffed up from a cold?" Generally, food just doesn't taste as good when you have a cold!

Describe what you smell

Mental Fitness Card 97

The activity on Mental Fitness Card 97 stimulates two parts of the brain by asking participants to bring together the sense of smell and the use of words. Encourage your group to be creative in their descriptions.

Thinking Card 71

Thinking Card 71 ("Describe What You Smell") has similar directions to Mental Fitness Card 97 but eliminates some information. Have some of the smells present so the group can smell, for example, a rose.

Smells and memories—scent associations

Mental Fitness Card 100

Now we're moving beyond describing smells to associating them with memories. When I describe "the smell of rain," I link it to my childhood home and watching the rain pour off the roof and sliding glass door. The rain fell on the tar-covered driveway, and in the summer the rain smelled like tar. Ask group members to talk about memories related to particular smells. Follow the directions on the card and remind them that this activity helps stimulate the area of the brain involved with both odors and emotions.

Thinking Card 72

Tea and coffee tasting

Most seniors come from the era of "coffee is coffee is coffee." They order either regular or decaf. Today, we have the opportunity to order not only specialty coffees, but a whole slew of exotic coffee drinks. I've been to coffee-tasting events and have also held them with seniors. It's great fun to have someone from a coffee shop come in to a senior center or residence. Or you can take a group to the local coffee shop and ask the staff to conduct a coffee-tasting event in-house. If you organize the tasting yourself, make sure you use many varieties of coffee. Using small cups for sampling, ask the participants to try to identify the tastes in the different coffees. You can also do this with teas.

Touching

The sense of touch is largely underdeveloped in American culture. This may be a result of too many no-no's as we were growing up, such as "Don't touch—it might break," or "Don't touch—it's dirty," or "Don't touch—that's naughty." We've also come to a point in our culture where touch has been misused, so we tend not to have *any* touch. Tell your group, "Older adults are some of the most touch-deprived people in our culture." Then ask, "Why do you think that is so?" I believe some of it is because we tend to see old as ugly. Or because some older adults have such fragile skin that others are afraid to touch them. In any case, here we're trying to rekindle what we had naturally as children—a desire to touch and an enjoyment of the way things feel. That's our goal with the next three activities.

Touch without looking

In numbered paper lunch sacks, place articles to be touched but not seen. Ask each person to write the numbers 1–12 on a piece of paper. As the sack is passed around, participants feel what's in it, then write down what they think it is. (No gooey stuff, please!) Here are some good objects to use: fur, pinecone, can opener, gourd, yarn, small brush, coins, buttons, coffee beans, pencil, paperclips and sand. Imagination is the guide to picking objects. Participants, if they are willing, can be responsible for setting up the activity. Some participants may have difficulty identifying objects they can't see. Take advantage of this circumstance to discuss why this is so.

Describe without naming

This is a variation on the previous activity. Ask participants to feel the objects in the sacks but to refrain from naming them. Instead ask them to write a short description of the object. In many ways, this is more challenging than naming objects.

The bread of life

Wind up the session with an activity that combines four of the five senses: Sight, smell, taste and touch. (We would include hearing, but it's hard to hear bread!) Provide each participant with a piece of bread. It's best to use homemade bread that is heavy in texture. Ask them to look at the bread, smell it, taste it and touch it in a deliberate and thoughtful way—and then to write about what they have experienced:

1. What does it look like? Color? Texture?

2. What does it smell like?

3. Describe the taste.

4. How does it feel?

5. Why is bread often referred to as "the staff of life?"

Homework

Encourage the group to be extra aware of smells by following the directions on Mental Fitness Card 99 ("Sniff Your Way Around").

Mental Fitness Card 99

seven

Participant Materials

Breathe, Breathe, Breathe

Mental Fitness Card 1

Breathing deeply is one of the most important things we can do to keep our minds mentally alert. Twenty percent of the air we breathe goes to our brain. Seniors are notoriously shallow breathers. Practice this breathing exercise as advocated by Dr. Andrew Weil on a daily basis and especially before doing a mental aerobic exercise.

You may want to do this sitting with your back straight, lying on your back, or standing or walking.

Exhale completely through the mouth, making an audible sound. Then, close the mouth and inhale quietly through the nose to a count of four. Hold the breath for a count of seven. Next, exhale audibly through the mouth to a count of eight. Repeat for a total of four cycles, then breathe normally.

The speed with which you do the exercise is unimportant. What is important is the ratio of four, seven, eight for inhalation, hold and exhalation.

Really Seeing

Mental Fitness Card 83

Vision is by far our most important sense. Some researchers estimate that about 90 percent of the information our brains receive comes through the eyes. Yet, we often look but we do not REALLY SEE. Looking is a generalized viewing; seeing is a keen visual awareness.

List on a piece of paper every object you see around you, from the largest item to the smallest detail. Give yourself plenty of time, looking carefully and listing as many items as you possibly can. Remember to list every little thing as well as larger things. You should have a very long list. Press yourself to add more and more details as you begin to REALLY SEE.

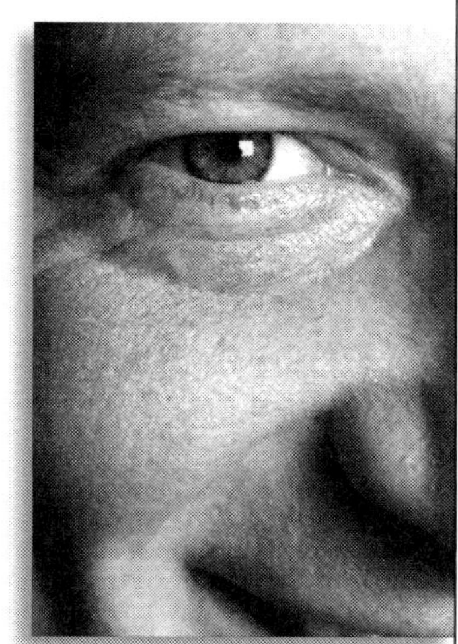

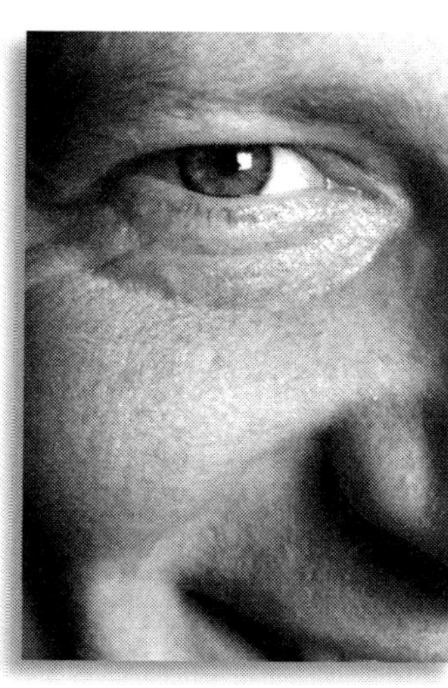

Really Seeing

Thinking Card 67

Some researchers estimate that about 90 percent of the information our brains receive comes through our eyes. However, we often look but don't REALLY SEE.

Seeing requires visual awareness.

List on paper or name every object you see around you, from the largest item to the smallest.

Give yourself plenty of time to look carefully.

What Is in Your Hand?

Mental Fitness Card 84

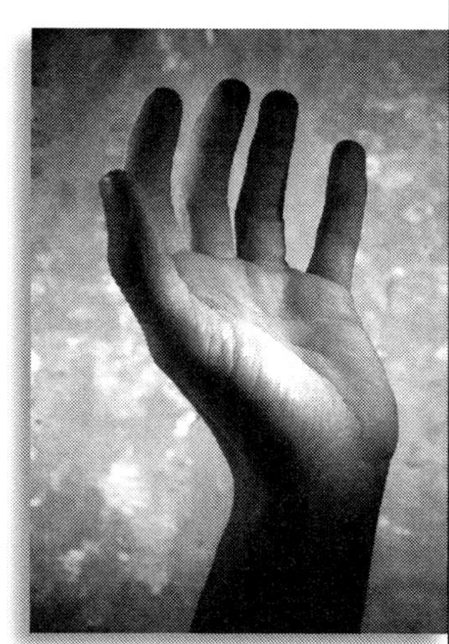

Look at your right hand. Look at the palm and trace with your finger the lines and furrows. Feel the texture of your skin. Is it soft, rough, dry, moist? Feel the flesh that cushions the bones. Feel the bones under the skin and flesh. Observe the veins on the back of the hand. Check out your fingernails. How would you describe their shape? Are there moons at the base of the nails?

Place one hand flat on a sheet of paper and trace around it with a pencil. Notice if your fingers are short or long. Is your hand long and slender or short and boxy? Look again at the lines in your palm. As you may know, there is a science of reading palms. If you are interested, try to get a book from the library about palm reading. It will be a wonderful brain exercise.

What Is in Your Hand?

Thinking Card 68

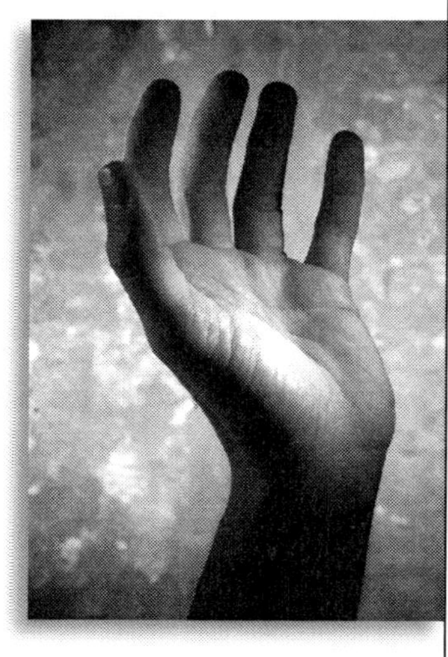

Look at your right hand.

Look at the palm and trace the lines and furrows with your finger.

Feel your skin. Is it soft, rough, dry, moist?

Observe the veins on the back of the hand.

Look at your fingernails.

Place one hand flat on a sheet of paper and trace around it with a pencil.

Are your fingers short or long? Is your hand long and slender or short and boxy? Take some time to really observe.

Sharpen Your Hearing

Mental Fitness Card 91

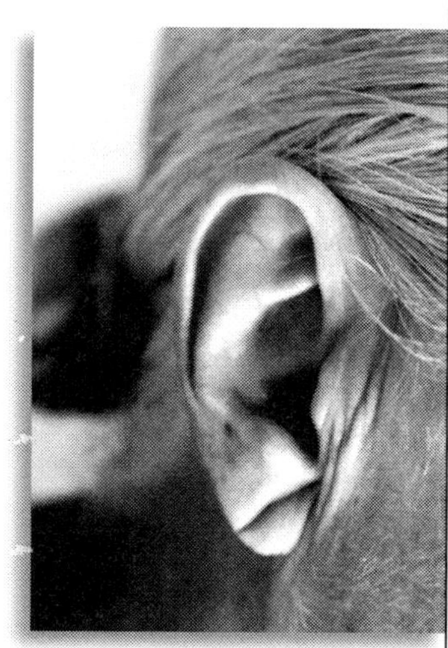

This activity is designed to help you sharpen your hearing and improve your concentration. Turn on the radio to a talk show or a news report. Lower the volume until it is just barely audible. Then, draw a horizontal line on a sheet of paper. Put the point of the pencil at the beginning of the line and very slowly turn up the volume of the radio. When you can understand clearly what is being said on the radio, make a mark on the line.

Repeat this activity several times in one day striving to make the mark on the paper earlier each time. Try the activity again several days later, each time working to hear the talking more clearly and sooner than the last time.

The change may not be dramatic, but you should notice some improvement as a result of purposeful listening and concentration.

Music and Mood

Thinking Card 99

We know that music affects our mood. Look through your collection of records, tapes or CDs. Choose four different songs that you enjoy which fit these moods:

Song 1: Slow, quiet and maybe a little melancholy.

Song 2: A bit peppier, but still tranquil and mellow.

Song 3: Faster tempo and more upbeat mood—a toe-tapper.

Song 4: Fast, lively and happy— makes you want to dance.

If you are feeling blue, try playing the songs in order, from 1 to 4. If you want to calm down and take a rest, play the songs in order from 4 to 1.

Describe What you Smell

Mental Fitness Card 97

It's not easy, but describing in words what we smell helps sensitize us to those smells. This activity brings together our sense of smell with the words that describe the smell and stimulates two different parts of the brain. Try to find one or two words to describe each of the following smells:

- the smell of rain

- the smell of burning leaves

- the smell of onions frying

- the smell of cabbage cooking

- the smell of a wet dog

- the smell of freshly mown hay

- the smell of newly cultivated soil

- the smell of a sweating body

- the smell of gasoline

- the smell of dirty hair

- the smell of a rose

Describe What You Smell

Thinking Card 71

It's not easy, but when we use words to describe what
we smell, we stimulate two different parts of the brain.
Try to find one or two words to describe each of the
following smells:

- the smell of rain

- the smell of burning leaves

- the smell of onions frying

- the smell of cabbage cooking

- the smell of a wet dog

- the smell of freshly mown hay

- the smell of newly cultivated soil

- the smell of a sweating body

- the smell of gasoline

- the smell of dirty hair

- the smell of a rose

Scent Associations

Mental Fitness Card 100

Write down in a column your five favorite smells.

Then, write down in a second column five smells you dislike the most.

Now, alongside each smell, write your associations with the favorite smells and then with the disliked smells.

As you reread what you have written, try to recapture in your memory what those smells were actually like.

When you do this, you are stimulating the area of the brain involved with odors and emotions.

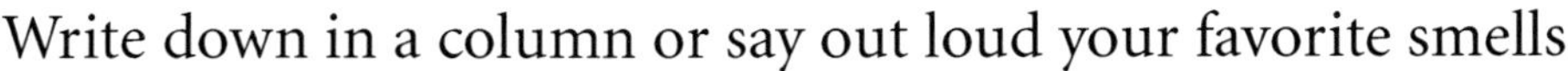

Scent Associations

Thinking Card 72

Write down in a column or say out loud your favorite smells.

Then, write down or tell what smells you dislike the most.

Is there something that each of these smells reminds you of? Write these down or talk about them with a friend or family member.

When you do this, you are stimulating the area of the brain involved with odors and emotions.

Sniff Your Way Around

Mental Fitness Card 99

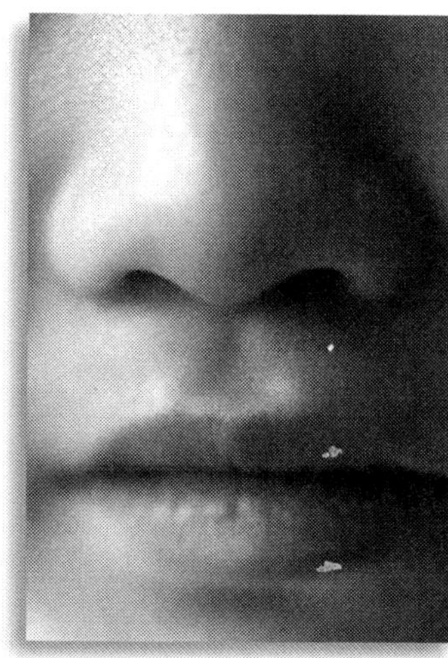

Smell is probably the sense we most underestimate. Of all of our senses, smell is the most basic. It is a chemical sense whose only requirement is that the chemical signal travels up the nose. Researchers tell us there are as many as 20 different odors.

Today, sniff your way around. Be extra aware of smells. Search out different smells. If you have a kitchen, go to the spice shelf and spend some time sniffing the different spices. If you are near a flower garden, take time to smell different flowers. If possible, go to a cosmetic counter and ask to smell different soaps and perfumes. You may want to find a restaurant that cooks different foods than you ordinarily eat and take time to be aware of different cooking odors. You will probably need to ask what you are smelling.

Get a pot of mint. It is a natural brain stimulant.

eight

Puzzling Out Puzzles and Numbers

eight

Puzzling Out Puzzles and Numbers

Goal

To use puzzles and numbers as mind stimulation.

Cards needed

Mental Fitness Cards 40, 41, 42, 68, 70, 71, 72, 73, 74, 78
Thinking Cards 59, 62, 96

Other resources

Flash cards, old math books, number lists, construction paper, posters, magazines, lightweight cardboard.

Supplies

Paper, pens/pencils, writing surfaces, overhead projector or bulletin board, scissors, glue.

Pertinent information

Researchers at the University of Minnesota Medical School learned that when persons in ice-cold rooms became thoroughly chilled and nothing could stop their teeth from chattering, the best warmer-upper was not a cup of hot coffee but a card brimming with rows of numbers to be added. Have you ever been aware, when you were struggling to balance your checkbook, that you began to feel warm? The reason, researchers speculate, is that when you do mental calculations, your breathing slows down and this makes you feel warmer.

Some of your group members may need a little extra encouragement when asked to work with numbers or puzzles. I was reluctant myself. I tend to claim, "I'm not a numbers person." I am naturally right-brained, but this means that I benefit greatly from working with numbers and puzzles that strengthen the left side of my brain. If you're caught in an emotional situation, doing some math problems can help you move quickly from the emotional side of your brain (the right side) to the intellectual side (your left brain). Try it some time!

Challenging the left brain

Mental Fitness Card 78

Give each participant a copy of Mental Fitness Card 78 and request that someone read the initial paragraph aloud. Ask the group: "How many of you remember doing story problems? And how many of you enjoy doing them?" This generally gets some chuckles and passionate talk about math failures. You may also want to ask, "How many of you use math and numbers on a daily basis?" When the conversation has died down, encourage participants to work the three story problems on this card.

Answers to Mental Fitness Card 78 ("Challenging the Left Brain")

1. Jane—3 miles
2. Sara—140 pounds
3. Ken—$195

COGNITIVE ADAPTATION

The instructions on Thinking Card 62 ("Challenging the Left Brain") are somewhat simpler than on Card 78, especially for Problem 2. This is, however, a challenging activity even to healthy older adults.

Thinking Card 62

Working some math problems

Mental Fitness Cards 40, 42

Make copies of Mental Fitness Cards 40 and 42 for everyone. When working Card 40, remind the group that there are two sides of the equation—the numbers on the left need to be added or subtracted to equal the number on the right. Those who aren't math-challenged tackle the problems on their own and sit quietly when they're finished. Meanwhile, groaning and moaning come from those who struggle, and they feel compelled to restate that they are "not math people." It's then I tell them they can work with each other. If you've got a number of frustrated people in your group, you can also remind them to employ breathing techniques to calm themselves. Our brains don't work well when we're trying too hard.

Answers to Mental Fitness Card 40 ("Addition and Subtraction")

$$3 + 2 - 1 + 4 - 1 + 3 = 10$$
$$8 - 7 + 1 + 4 + 4 - 6 = 4$$
$$5 - 3 + 2 + 4 + 1 + 5 = 14$$
$$2 - 1 + 8 + 9 - 3 + 5 = 20$$
$$5 - 3 + 4 - 4 - 2 + 9 = 9$$
$$7 - 6 + 2 + 9 - 9 - 3 = 0$$

Remembering numbers

Use "Remembering Numbers," the reproducible on page 158, or write two sets of six numbers on the flip chart or overhead projector, such as:

2, 4, 8, 3, 2, 5

and

6, 3, 9, 4, 5, 7

Ask participants to read these two sets of numbers over at least three times and then write them down in the correct order. If this proves too difficult for your group members, try writing only five numbers in each set. Ask participants to develop their own sets of numbers and keep practicing until their memory gets sharper. Assure them that practice does make a difference. In most cases, it's hard to memorize only because the brain is out of practice. Also remind participants to breathe and relax as they memorize.

Connecting the dots

Mental Fitness Card 68

Give each participant a copy of Mental Fitness Card 68 and ask for a volunteer to read the instructions aloud. After they've worked at connecting the dots without lifting their pencils, ask the group, "What restrictions have you set up for yourself in solving this problem?" Then reread the directions, emphasizing that there are no boundaries as to where the lines can be drawn. (In other words, they *can* draw outside the box.) Display the problem on a flip chart or overhead projector and draw the four lines for them. (If someone has figured it out, please have *them* draw the answer if they are willing and able.) Unless the members of your group have tried this puzzle before, they will struggle intensely to follow the directions. This can lead to a discussion on why we tend to stay "within the box."

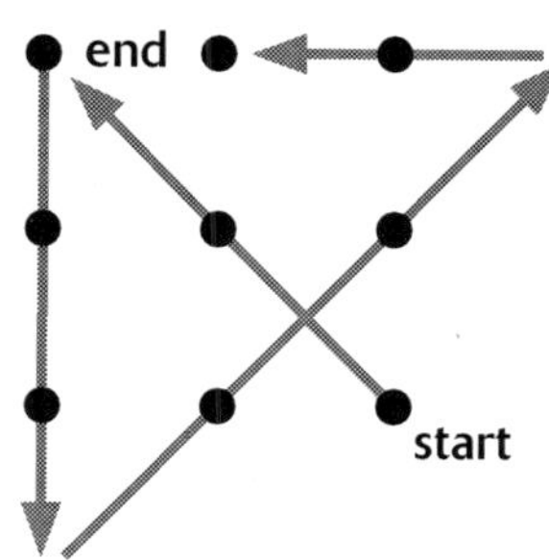

Answer to Mental Fitness Card 68 ("Connecting the Dots")

Coin puzzle

Mental Fitness Card 74

Gather enough pennies for each member of the group to work the puzzle. You can also break up a big group and have smaller groups work this puzzle. Again, ask someone to read the directions aloud.

Answer to Mental Fitness Card 74 ("Coin Puzzle")

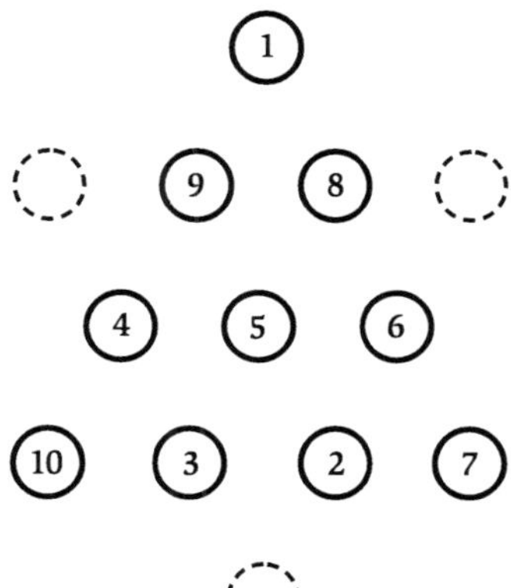

Jigsaw puzzle

Mental Fitness Card 71

Puzzles are great for exercising the part of the brain that deals with spatial perceptions. And it's almost addicting to sit down and "put a few pieces in." If you can get pictures of participants' families beforehand and create meaningful puzzles out of the photos for each group member, you'll be delighted with their response. I realize that this takes preparation time on your part. Here are easier ways to make jigsaw puzzles:

1. Cut up five-inch hearts or shamrocks into five or six pieces.

2. Cut letters from a large poster into puzzle pieces.

3. Paste magazine pictures on lightweight cardboard and cut them up.

Involve one group in creating puzzles and the other in putting them together. Then switch. Of course, intriguing commercial puzzles are widely available as well.

COGNITIVE ADAPTATION:

Commercial puzzles can be frustrating even to those of us without any cognitive challenges! I suggest you use Thinking Card 59 ("Jigsaw Puzzle"), especially if you can get pictures of the family. Software for making puzzles is available on the computer (puzzlesgalore.com is one source).

Breathing break

Before you move into counting, get the participants to take in some good, deep, relaxing breaths and clear their brains for the next challenge.

Counting

If you've ever taken a "mini-mental exam," you know one of the initial questions is, "Count backwards from 100 by sevens to zero." Most of us growl, but others start listing the numbers. Remind participants that the important part is exercising the brain, not getting the numbers right.

COGNITIVE ADAPTATION

Thinking Card 96 ("Counting Games") is a wonderful alternative to counting backward from 100 by sevens. Have the group warm up by counting up to 20 by twos, then threes, etc. Follow the directions on this enjoyable card.

Homework

For Mental Fitness Card 70, participants will need matchsticks (the wooden ones are best). For Cards 72 and 73, they will need only a copy of the card. If they're struggling with Card 72, encourage them to build the pyramid with blocks or sugar cubes.

These puzzles can also be done with grandchildren or friends. Remind the group to "Have fun challenging your brain!" Remind them that "Doing puzzles with grandchildren or other young friends can be oodles of fun."

Answer to Mental Fitness Card 70 ("Matchsticks")

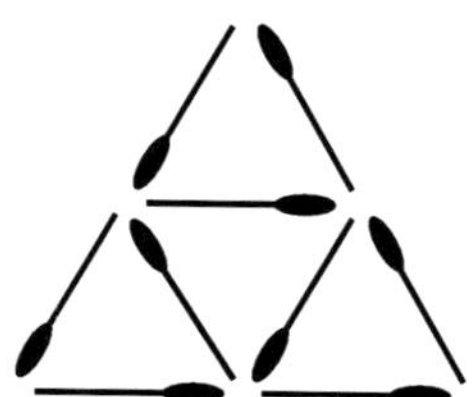

Answer to Mental Fitness Card 72 ("Hidden Cubes")

There are 31 total cubes, with 16 entirely hidden from view.

Answer to Mental Fitness Card 73 ("Triangles")

The figure has 35 triangles.

Challenging the Left Brain

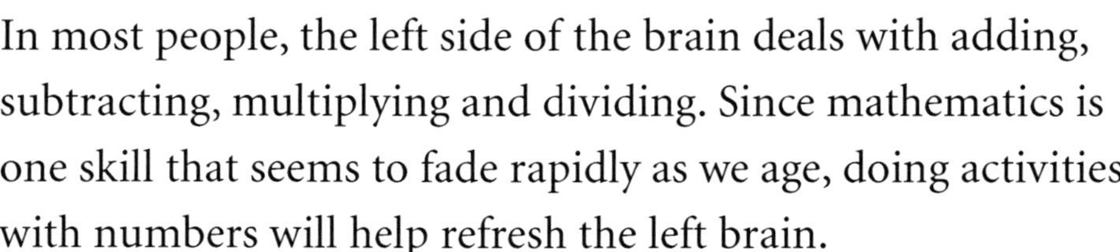

Mental Fitness Card 78

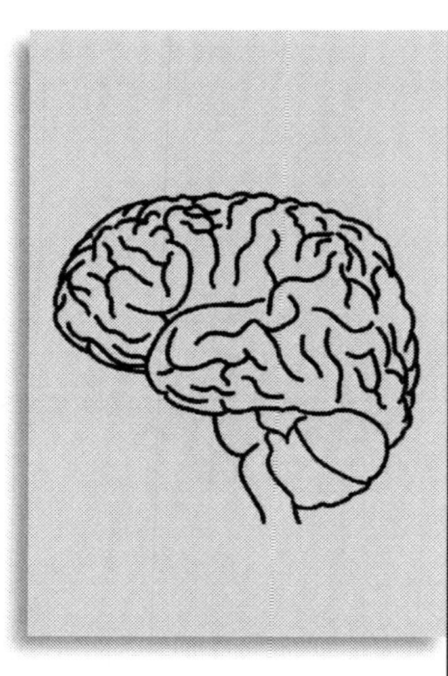

In most people, the left side of the brain deals with adding, subtracting, multiplying and dividing. Since mathematics is one skill that seems to fade rapidly as we age, doing activities with numbers will help refresh the left brain.

1. Jane walks a half mile in 15 minutes.
   How far will she have gone in 1½ hours?

2. Sara was 5 feet, 6 inches tall. When she weighed herself one day, she weighed 170 pounds. She was disturbed and put herself on a diet for 10 weeks. She lost 3 pounds each week. How much did she weigh at the end of the 10 weeks?

3. Ken was raising money to help build a children's playground. His neighbor gave him $20, his cousin gave him $40, his four children each gave him $15 and he added $75 from his own savings. How much did Ken collect?

Challenging the Left Brain

Thinking Card 62

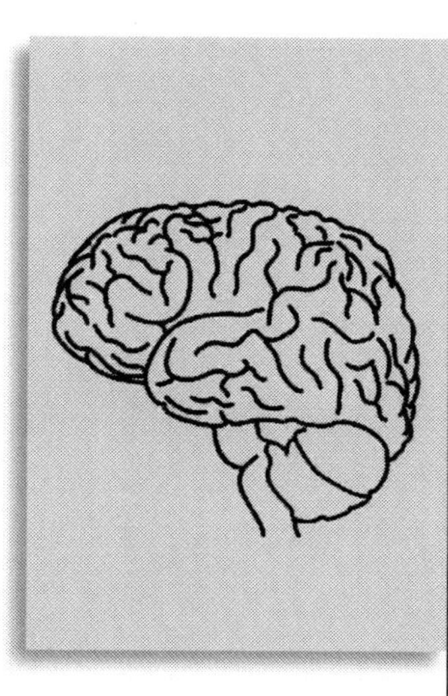

If you enjoy doing math, this might be a fun activity for you. In most people, the left side of the brain deals with adding, subtracting, multiplying and dividing. Since mathematics is one skill that seems to fade rapidly as we age, doing activities with numbers will help refresh the left brain.

1. Jane walks a half mile in 15 minutes. How far will she walk in 1½ hours?

2. Sara weighed 170 pounds and dieted for 10 weeks. She lost 3 pounds each week. How much did she weigh at the end of the 10 weeks?

3. Ken was raising money to help build a playground. His neighbor gave him $20, his cousin gave him $40, his four children each gave him $15 and he added $75 from his own savings. How much did Ken collect?

Addition and Subtraction

Mental Fitness Card 40

Place a + (plus) or a – (minus) sign between the digits
so that both sides of each equation are equal.

3	2	1	4	1	3	=	10
8	7	1	4	4	6	=	4
5	3	2	4	1	5	=	14
2	1	8	9	3	5	=	20
5	3	4	4	2	9	=	9
7	6	2	9	9	3	=	0

If you like this activity, invent some equations of your own.

Adding Numbers

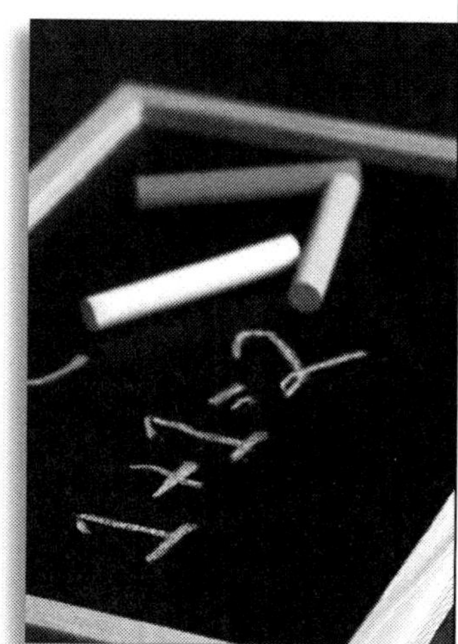

Mental Fitness Card 42

Replace each dot below with either 1, 2, 4, 5 or 6 to make the problem add up correctly. Each number may be used only once.

```
    5   •   •   •
    8   7   4   3
  ─────────────────
  1   •   3   5   •
```

Remembering Numbers

2 4 8 3 2 5

6 3 9 4 5 7

Connecting the Dots

Mental Fitness Card 68

Without lifting your pencil from the paper, draw four straight, connected lines which go through all nine dots but through each only once. After you have tried two different ways, ask yourself what restrictions you have set up for yourself in solving this problem. Be sure to read these directions several times.

Coin Puzzle

Mental Fitness Card 74

Arrange 10 coins to make this triangle. By moving only three coins, turn the triangle upside down.

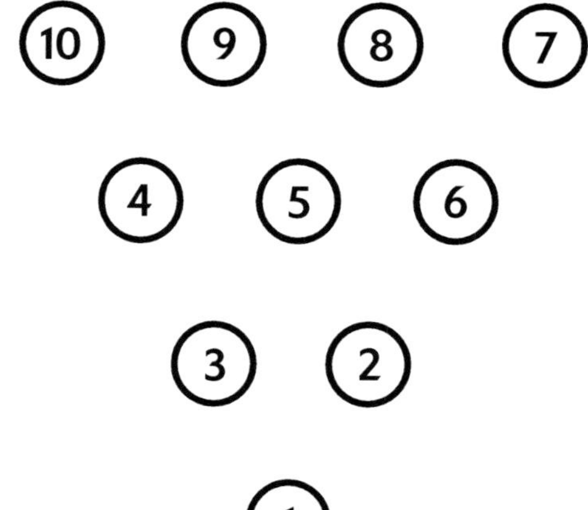

Jigsaw Puzzle

Mental Fitness Card 71

Jigsaw puzzles of any kind are a challenge to the part of the brain that deals with spatial perceptions. Make a puzzle by drawing this T shape on a piece of heavy paper and cutting it up into four pieces.

Now without looking at the original of the puzzle, put it back together. Put the pieces away for a week or more and try it again. Try it with friends. Other puzzles to make:

- A five inch heart cut into six pieces

- Letters from a large poster cut into puzzle pieces

- Pictures from a magazine pasted on heavy paper and cut up

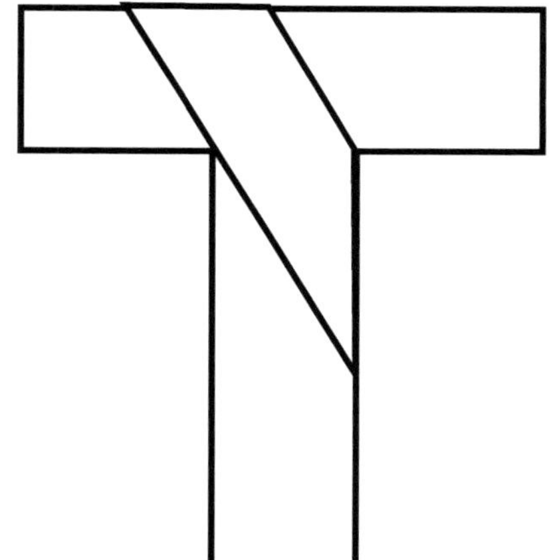

Jigsaw Puzzle

Thinking Card 59

Jigsaw puzzles of any kind are a challenge to the part of the brain that deals with spatial perceptions.

You or a family member can make your own jigsaw puzzles by cutting photos or magazine pictures into anywhere from four to six pieces. Then try to put the pieces together to form the whole picture.

Instead of making your own puzzle, you can also purchase puzzles with different levels of difficulty.

Even simple puzzles are good for the brain!

Counting

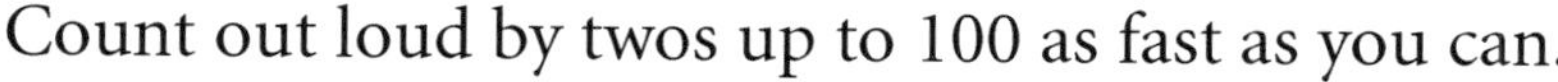

Mental Fitness Card 41

Count out loud by twos up to 100 as fast as you can.

Count backward by twos from 100 to zero.

Now try counting by threes up to 100.

Now count backward by threes from 100.

For the ultimate challenge, count forward by sevens and then count backward by sevens.

Counting Games

Thinking Card 96

Do you remember when you learned your multiplication facts in school? You may have learned to count by twos, threes, fours, etc.

Try counting by threes:

3 ... 6 ... 9 ... 12 ... 15 ... 18 ...

How far can you go?

Now try counting by other numbers.

If you want a real challenge, try to list the prime numbers. (Prime numbers are divisible only by one and themselves.) To help you get started:

1 ... 3 ... 5 ... 7 ... 11 ... 13 ...

Can you continue?

Matchsticks

Mental Fitness Card 70

Arrange nine matchsticks in a triangle as shown. Now, rearrange five of the matchsticks so that there are a total of five triangles.

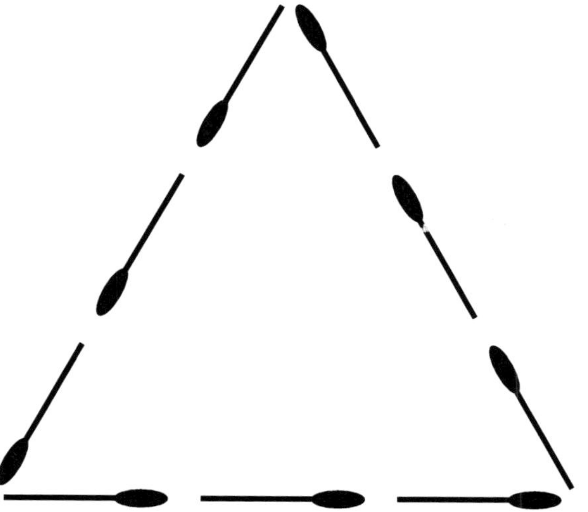

Hidden Cubes

Mental Fitness Card 72

How many cubes are there in all? How many cubes are entirely hidden and cannot be seen?

Count the number of triangles found in this drawing. It may be helpful to number the small areas and then write down the combinations that make up all the different triangles.

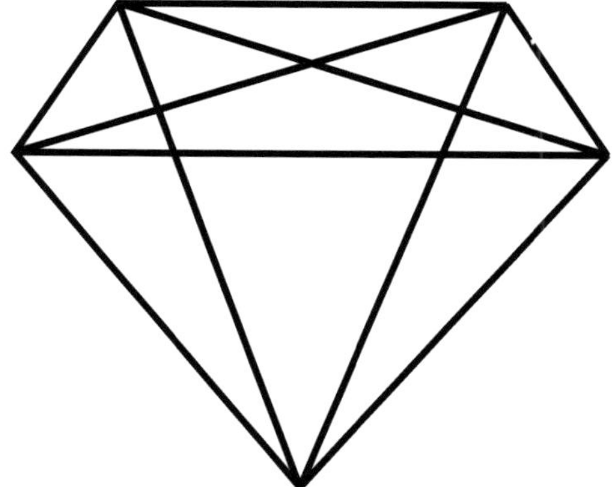